B9363

RENFREW COUN

HEADQUARTERS: March

CARE OF BOOKS. Readers are ask
  books in their possession.

TIME ALLOWED FOR READING. Books may be retained for two
  weeks, and are due for return not later than the latest date
  stamped below. A fine of one penny will be charged for every
  three days the book is kept beyond the time allowed.

RENEWALS. A loan may be extended if the book is not required by
  another reader.

16. OCT 1967
30. OCT. 1967

12. JUL. 1968

26. JUL. 1974

NOT TO BE W/D
S U C
23.3.81.

AG LTD

CHRONICLE OF THE
WORKER-PRIESTS

CHRONICLE
OF THE
WORKER-PRIESTS

Translated and edited by

STANLEY WINDASS

THE MERLIN PRESS
LONDON

CONTENTS

Preface

TEN YEARS ago we were in the thick of the conflict over the worker-priests. It was a conflict which shook public opinion, and had repercussions in France, Belgium, and Italy, far beyond the circle of those normally concerned with the Church's affairs.

These pioneers of the missionary apostolate had profoundly moved the consciences of men. Some they had shaken rudely out of their comfortable routines; others had felt their deeply rooted prejudices being undermined. Even in the working class itself, which was believed to be, and which believed itself to be, foreign to the Church and to religion, a confused hope had been born, when these men, marked by the Church with the sign of the Priesthood as ministers of Christ, had made up their minds to share completely the work and life of the proletariat, in order to bring their Lord to the midst of the people. There were only a handful of them, these new missionaries—a hundred or so in the whole of France, lost amongst the seething masses of the factories, the workshops, the sprawling industrial suburbs. . . . They sought no publicity, preferring to work out their vocations in obscurity; but they were men who had joined the ranks of the spiritually disinherited with unmistakable proofs of their sincerity and of the reality of their commitment.

Not only did they adopt the way of life and the poverty

7

of the proletariat, but they took the unprecedented step of committing themselves fully to factory labour and to all that it involved; they had promised to their comrades in the workshops, in the docks, on the building sites, that they would henceforth share to the full their material hardships and their legitimate moral aspirations, without keeping open any escape route to the *bourgeoisie*, where they were supposed to 'belong'.

The bishops, on the other hand, who had authorized and encouraged these exceptional vocations, imparted to their enterprise that necessary degree of caution and prudence which made it genuinely an act of the Church, a mission conferred on them by the hierarchy to be carried out in the name of the entire Christian community. Cardinal Suhard was already a leader of the movement before he became fully and officially responsible for its direction as Cardinal-Archbishop of Paris, and it was he who defined its task: there was a chasm between the Church of Christ, the Redeemer of all mankind, and the working-class; a chasm which no one had been able to cross—not even Catholic Action, for all its generous initiatives; where laymen had failed, the worker-priests should now make their effort to succeed, by simply bringing the divine presence to the world of the disinherited.

It was not a provisional experiment, or a secret tactical manœuvre. It was a meaningful act, like that of the missionary who renounces once and for all his country, his people, his culture, to become a different being, a Gentile among the Gentiles. It was a living witness, in a land where the preaching of the Word was still impossible; it was a burial within the meal of the leaven of priestly prayer.

After the death of the pastor who had fostered this new form of mission, the cardinals and archbishops of France, especially those of the industrial cities, who shared the same longings, remained loyal to the enterprise, fully appreciating the risks that were involved and the prize that was to be won; they kept in the closest possible contact with the worker-priests, though it was sometimes difficult to give them adequate direction and support.

In the autumn of 1953, it began to be rumoured abroad that instructions had come from Rome to stop the 'experiment' of the worker-priests. In January 1954, every worker-priest received a personal letter from his bishop instructing him to renounce full-time work, since the joining together of these two states of life, that of a priest and that of a worker, was 'damaging the very idea of the priesthood'.

The decision immediately aroused the most violent criticism —for the way in which it had emanated from the supreme authority (Pius XII) via the Holy Office, for the way it was transmitted to the worker-priests, for its appearance of a verdict passed on the conduct of ministers of Christ whose generosity had commanded the respect of the whole of France. The commentaries were not always well-informed —the inquisitorial methods of the Holy Office do not assist the flow of accurate information—but their passionate nature was a measure of the hope which had been placed in these new apostles.

Since that time, though interest has not waned (witness the success of Monsignor Ancel's recently published book), passion has given way to uncertainty. The meaning of what happened was not well understood—partly because it was difficult to follow accurately the history of the movement, and partly because it is hard to grasp the nature of the religious and social problems which are involved.

It is therefore particularly appropriate that we should have those documents readily available which help to throw light on this recent and still confused period of history.

As its title suggests, this book is a *chronicle*; it is a calendar

9

of events, and a collection of documents reflecting the experiences and sufferings of the worker-priests, the pastoral concern of the Church, the commentaries of witnesses, the views of outsiders.

All these provide material for reflection. The author helps us to understand both sides of the conflict. It would have been easy for him to stir up the embers of recent passions; but he preferred to put us on our guard, by his own example, against the summary judgements which are so frequently pronounced.

Hasty judgements were made in the crisis of 1953-4. Some put the blame on the imprudence of the worker-priests, on their partisanship, on their 'progressivism'—forgetting that 'the Church has always respected the purity of their intentions and the extraordinary generosity of their actions' (Mgr. Ancel). Others blamed the lack of contact between bishops and worker-priests, ignoring the continued concern of the bishops of France which is so evident in these pages. Others placed the whole responsibility on the rigour of the Holy See, which was cut off from the realities of the working-class, and excessively influenced by powerful social pressures —without admitting that the Church has continuously said that she seeks new paths for the working-class apostolate, which is still her most urgent concern. The documents which are collected here help to correct these overhasty judgements.

During the long debate between the worker-priests and the bishops, and between the highest representatives of the French hierarchy and the Holy See, the fundamental question was one which must recur periodically in the missionary work of the Church: how can the priest at once identify himself with a society which is a stranger to revelation, and at the same time lead a full priestly life, according to the mind of Christ and the tradition of the Church?

As we read the well-documented account presented to

us here, we can usefully reflect on this perennial problem. We are not just concerned to revive old memories; as we pay homage to the courage of these pioneer apostles, we shall, I think, come to realize two principles which must now be accepted by all thinking Catholics:

(1) It is now more vital than ever that ways should be found to replace the worker-priests and to continue their mission. The Church has continued her efforts to make contact with the world of the workers; she was at work in 1954, and she continues to work today, through the Missionary Brothers, the *Petits Frères de Jesus* the *Frères du Prado* an organization whose admirable work is sometimes little appreciated by the public. Nevertheless, 'the world of the workers is still waiting'; this is the judgement of Monsignor Ancel, the bishop who has participated most directly in the apostolate of work. It is waiting for the Church to come to it, as a sociological reality—it is waiting for priests to make the love of God present within it in a way it can understand.

(2) The working-class is a world de-Christianized by its very conditions of work and by the industrial régime, and its evangelization is the responsibility of the entire Catholic community. Nothing could be more inappropriate than to applaud from afar, like a spectator, or to sit in judgement, like a historian, over those who took the risks and embraced the vocations which are the most urgent requirement of our time. The worker-priests needed the support of a virile Catholic Action, of a laity dedicated to the working-class mission, of parishes which were open and welcoming to them —in short of a body of *faithful*, with the tenacious will that that word should imply to cling both to the Church and to the world to which the Church would bring salvation. The evangelization of the working-class will not be accomplished by a few private efforts, by a few heroic adventures, but, as

11

one of the leaders of the Church in France has put it, 'by the united work of all apostles, priests, religious and laymen, inspired and directed by the bishops, to whom the missionary preaching of the Word of God is first entrusted'.

André Latreille
Dean of the Faculty of Letters, Lyons

Introduction

JEAN FOLLIET distinguished three main stages in the evolution of contemporary French Catholicism; these he called Social Catholicism, Specialized Catholic Action, and the Missionary Movement. The worker-priests came from the fiery centre of the missionary movement. In 1958, Monsignor Garrone wrote in his book on Catholic Action, 'The history of the worker-priests has left on the heart of the Church and on the minds of many believers and non-believers a festering wound which has scarcely healed, and which is always ready to re-open; but this is not the place to repeat the story of that bold experiment, and the great generosity of those who took part in it, or to examine the reasons for its interruption'.[1]

These words are typical of the embarrassed reserve with which the worker-priest issue is still treated today. It is the result of shame, of respect, and of fear: shame, for the violence and passion which were involved; respect, for those who could be harmed by indiscretion; fear, for the brood of polemists who thrive on the stench of scandal and disorder.

Yet this embarrassed reserve is harmful both to Christians and to non-Christians; for they simply do not know what happened. How many times, in the course of discussions on the Church, the same questions crop up, among the workers and among the *bourgeoisie*, among the young and the old:

[1] See page 109.

13

'What do you make of the worker-priests? Did they really betray the Church? Did the Church betray them?' People want to know the truth; they wish to make a well-informed judgement of this exceptionally courageous missionary enterprise, because they suspect that one day the problems that have been temporarily pushed underground will again have to be faced. Progress is made through experiments, mistakes, reform; grace ultimately triumphs, and the Light eventually drives away the darkness. People want to know what happened, because they are secretly convinced that it was not so much an 'apostolic aberration' as the painful birth of something new, which will eventually find its place, in a more enlightened, more mature, and purer form, in the immense task of bringing Christ to the modern world.

For this reason we have gathered together in this book, as faithfully as possible, a record of all the events, decisions, points of view from all sides which can help to reconstitute the problem in its full historical reality. It is quite probable that some of those who were closely involved in the conflict would no longer, after this interval of time, speak in quite the same language. They reacted spontaneously with the light that they then had, and with all the passion which moved them at the time; we must not judge their attitudes with the superior wisdom of hindsight. This book has no polemical character, and no other purpose than to collect together a number of documents in the service of history; for today this should be a matter of history, and not of polemics. We take sides neither for nor against the worker-priests; and this is not out of prudence, but out of respect for the judgement of Father Finet :

'Whether we like it or not, two opposed mentalities, and two opposed societies, confront each other; and it is far too easy a solution to say that one represents the mind of Christ, and the other has "gone astray".'

14

For other reasons too it is a mistake to make mass-judgements. In the first place, although the condemnation applies generally to all worker-priests, when it comes to giving an accurate account of their experiences distinctions have always to be made, for the group was by no means homogeneous; even on essential points, the worker-priests were often in disagreement. One has therefore to speak of *'a certain number of the worker priests'*, or *'the majority of the worker-priests'*. . . .

In the second place, a great deal of passion has been spent on this issue. Not only in France, but in other countries too, people have taken up arms on one side or the other over this small group of priests; it has become something of a national scandal, 'a second Dreyfus affair', as François Mauriac put it. There have been secret manœuvres on both sides, and often we seem to be groping in the dark.

Cardinal Saliège said quite rightly, 'It is just as if there is a co-ordinated campaign, orchestrated periodically by certain organs of the Press, and by more or less secret meetings, tending to prepare in the bosom of the Church a welcome for Communism. There are in this campaign those who lead and know, and those who follow but do not know.' There is no doubt that the worker-priests were subjected to Communist pressure.

On the other hand, Etienne Borne wrote at about the same time, and with equal justification, 'There are in existence professional denunciation agencies, maintained by certain business circles which cover their dedication to capitalist interests with the cloak of religious piety. These so-called "integralists" are at the moment priding themselves publicly on winning a victory over the French hierarchy and the tradition of Cardinal Suhard.'[2]

The integralist pressure on the ecclesiastical authorities

[2] *La Vie Intellectuelle,* April 1954.

matched the Communist pressure on the worker-priests. Openly or in secret, everyone was caught up in passionate conflict.

Initiatives of non-Roman Catholic Christian bodies complicated the issues even further. On the 24th June 1959, Cardinal Pizzardo announced that the Holy Office had decided that priests 'must cease to work as employees in factories or as sailors on fishing or transport vessels'. Five months later, the Anglican Church launched an experiment similar to that of the worker-priests. A number of Anglican clerical students assembled in a centre in Birmingham to work full-time as factory hands, meeting in the evenings to meditate together on the experiences of the day; the Anglican bishop, a former prisoner of the Japanese, considered that this experiment was necessary to understand the lives of men in the modern world and to bring the gospel effectively to them.

To sum up, we shall endeavour first of all to present *the facts* as fully as possible. Then this historical introduction will serve as a framework within which we shall study the problems raised by the events. Here we shall examine in turn the problems which faced the worker-priests; the solutions which they found, the reactions of the hierarchy; the attempted re-adjustments, and the second condemnation; and, finally, the basic problems which still remain.[3]

[3] The Church did in fact suppress the term 'worker-priest', quite apart from the movement itself. We nevertheless continue to use the term in this book, since it is a historical study.

CHAPTER I

Origins

BEFORE THE 1914-1918 war, a Frenchman by the name of Jacques Vaudour had adopted the life of a worker in order to study at first hand the problems of the urban and rural proletariat. He was so struck by the de-Christianization of the masses that he started the tradition of regarding France as a new mission-territory.

1926:

The Young Christian Workers was founded. This was the first mass-movement for the evangelization of the working-class.

1929:

Monsignor Suhard, Bishop of Bayeux, told a young seminarian : 'There is a whole country around Caen, containing all our great factories, where Christ is unknown; this is our true mission-land. Day and night this thought is in my mind. I long for missionaries.'

1939:

Professor Le Bras began to apply sociological techniques to the study of religious practice.

Father Adrian Bosquet, a Franciscan from Toulouse, was sent by his provincial at Ivry to study the problem of the working-class in a large factory. He worked in collaboration with two other members of religious orders.

17

1940:

Jacques Loew went to work as a docker at Marseilles, in collaboration with a group called *Economie et Humanisme.* Born in 1908, he was a graduate in Law and Political Science, converted at the age of 24, and ordained priest in the Dominican Order in 1939.

1941:

Eight hundred thousand Frenchmen were deported to work in Germany, and the German authorities refused to allow chaplains to accompany them. Monsignor Rodhain, chaplain-general for prisoners-of-war, in agreement with Cardinal Suhard, secretly sent twenty-five priests among the workers. Twenty-four were arrested, and of these two died in concentration camps. In this group of workers, Father Dillard reported later that he found no trace of religious concern; in the midst of dreadful dangers, no one was in the least troubled about spiritual matters. They were hardly even surprised by the sacrifices of the volunteer worker-priests; they regarded their talk of the life to come as a sort of clerical trick to get hold of people—rather like the insurance agent's talk about the danger of fire. 'They don't want our merchandise, because they cannot see its use,' remarked Father Dillard. 'When I come home in the evening exhausted by the day's work, I am obsessed with this problem : what am I to do? what can I say to them? I am a stranger, I belong to another culture. My Latin, my liturgy, my theology, my mass, my prayers, my vestments, all help to make me an object of curiosity, something set apart, like a strange lingering survivor of an archaic cult.'

Father Perrin noticed the same things : 'They do not know the priest; they are separated from him by a great gulf. We do not belong to the same world'. Like Father

Dillard, he found the need for a more evangelical form of Christianity. Before we think about the pagan world, they said, we have to think about the Christian world, and about the ecclesiastical world. Among the workers they found about 1 to 2 per cent practising Catholics—scouts, Y.C.W. members, seminarians. These were 'timid and reticent in the face of real life; instead of acting like men in the service of Christ, they groaned under the hardships, resigned themselves grudgingly, and gradually let bitterness and rancour gather in their hearts. Their faith did not call forth their vitality. Their interior lives were only a grasping and feeble kind of contentment, which aggravated their only too common physical debility; a self-protective kind of spirituality, exercises of piety by which they could isolate themselves and hold off the turbulent world which surged around them and threatened to overwhelm them. They were content to keep together in their little groups; they had nothing to give to the world which was dying before their eyes.'

Father Perrin was horrified to see Christianity so turned in on itself, when faced with such a challenge. How was it that people nourished for years on the sacraments, with all the religious formation of the seminaries and the Catholic Action movements, could so shirk their responsibilities? He saw that Christianity must be prepared to lose in conformity in order to gain in vitality; he felt the need for a new kind of Christian community—'A hard life, a high degree of communal living; initiation to service of all kinds and to a sense of collective and personal responsibility; some form of frequent confession; the awakening of a personal religion; first-hand experience of every kind of environment'.[1] Only by reading the diary of this worker-priest in Germany can one receive the full impact of his radical religious thought. He was convinced that priests would have to enter the

[1] Editions de la Bonne Presse.

factories as workers when the war was over; laymen would not be enough. His writing also suggests a new orientation for the Y.C.W. and *The Way*.

1942:

A seminary called the Mission de France opened at Lisieux. This was the realization of a plan which Cardinal Suhard had worked on throughout the long years of his episcopate; a seminary dedicated specifically to the education of missionary priests, to work among the de-Christianized masses of the under-manned dioceses. Among the first students at the Mission was the Abbé Godin, already ordained, a former Fils de la Charité and a Y.C.W. chaplain.

Abbé Godin, a 'man of providence', in the words of Father Glorieux,[2] was born in 1906, on Good Friday, in the town of Le Doubs. He left a humble family to become the apostle of the poor; he left a village of only a hundred inhabitants to become a real Parisian of the suburbs. He was highly intelligent, generous, human, dynamic, and extremely unconventional; he had worked as a Y.C.W. chaplain in the 18th *arrondissement* of Paris, where in 1942 there were four Y.C.W. sections with less than a hundred members, only thirty of whom were active, out of a population of 30,000 young workers. Among the active members were a few real saints; Godin knew this, and he loved the Y.C.W. But many Jocists, once they were married, dropped out of the movement altogether. Abbé Godin, with his companion Abbé Daniel, studied closely the ways of life of the proletariat, and realized that religion must be stripped of its *bourgeois* trappings and made incarnate in working-class thought and action. The Y.C.W. he felt had failed to come to grips with the working masses, because it was too much bound to the old parishes, and too much dominated by their spirit. The problem had already been raised some years before by

[2] Editions de la Bonne Presse

20

Maxence van der Meersch's novel, *Pêcheurs d'Hommes*. Abbé Godin saw too that the Y.C.W. chaplains were very poorly prepared for this special task; they were parish clergy, often far removed from the working-class, and overloaded with other work, in a way that made them quite inadequate to meet the demands of the time. He looked forward to a time when there would be a clergy specially trained for and dedicated to the working-class, who could be present even where the Church was absent, and help to build new communities which would be at once truly proletarian and truly Christian.

Abbé Godin wrote to Cardinal Suhard about his ideas; the cardinal was so excited by the letter that he stayed up all night reading it, for it harmonized with his own deep pastoral concerns. When he was enthroned as archbishop of Paris, he had said, 'In view of the de-Christianization which has taken place during the past thirty years, have we any right to be satisfied with acquired positions? Is it not obvious that simply to keep what we have is to lose all, to slither down a slope towards total apostasy, and total ruin?' In 1943, Abbé Godin published his book, *France, Pays de Mission?*[3] He had already published, the year before, his new missal, *Avec le Christ*,[4] specially adapted for the working-class environment, with a new style and layout; 1943 also saw the appearance of his fine collection, *Le Levain dans la Pâte*,[5] which was aimed at making theology incarnate in real life.

France, Pays de Mission? made a powerful impact. Christian groups who had been less aware of the problem than Cardinal Suhard suddenly woke up; the abbé soon found enthusiastic supporters, as well as some opponents. Part of the Y.C.W., and certain Christian and trade union political movements, complained that he had not taken

Editions du Cerf, 1943. [4] Editions Ouvrières. [5] Editions Ouvrières.

21

sufficient account of their influence in the body of the
working-class.

In any case, it was less than a year before Abbé Godin's
ideas bore fruit in the foundation of the Mission de Paris.
Abbé Michonneau was asked by Cardinal Suhard to
become its superior, but he refused, because he wanted to
continue with his work of transforming the parish of Sacré-
Coeur de Colombes into a 'missionary community'. The
cardinal therefore approached Abbé Hollande, a priest from
the suburbs, who accepted the post in October 1943. The
Mission de Paris had at that time six members, including
Abbé Godin and Abbé Daniel. On the 15th January 1944,
the first priests of the Mission dedicated themselves, before
the Blessed Virgin, to work for the Christianization of the
working-class of Paris, according to the judgement of the
missionary community, during the period in which they
should remain in its service.

Abbé Godin could hardly believe that his wishes had been
so miraculously fulfilled : 'Now,' he said, 'the Mission can
live without me'. On the next day, he was found dead
in his humble room at No. 47, rue Ganneron; the stove
had set fire to his bedding during the night. Perhaps he had
slept too soundly after working far into the night; perhaps
he had failed to awaken because of heart failure, due to the
accumulated fatigue of years of labour.

The Mission was, of course, crippled by the loss of its
guiding light. To understand how things developed during
the following years, we must first see exactly what was in
the abbé's mind.

(1) In the first place, the Mission was conceived from the
beginning as an extra-parochial organization. Like his
intimate friend, Father Michonneau, Abbé Godin believed
firmly in the necessity of a reform of the parishes, which
was then just beginning to get under way. But the large

parishes which served the working-class areas had not yet begun to think about reform, and he could not wait until this process was complete before starting on his apostolate of the masses. At the same time, since his experience as a curate at Clichy, he was more attracted to missionary work outside the parish system; and in this respect there is a difference of orientation between the Mission de Paris and the Mission de Marseilles, where Father Loew became a parish-priest (at La Cabucelle) in 1947 while he was still employed as a factory-worker.[6]

(2) Abbé Godin was not in any sense the founder of the worker-priests. He simply wished to form little groups of priests entirely detached from the parish ministry and free to explore every possible means of making contact with the workers. Abbé Daniel, who was his collaborator from the beginning, confirms that he never even thought about the idea of worker-priests. What his future thoughts would have been is hard to determine; but we know that he once said, 'Why should I ever leave off my *soutane*, when the whole day is insufficient for my work?'

(3) Still less then did he ever think of priests taking a part in trade union activity. Abbé Daniel, who knew him intimately, is certain that, because of his exclusively priestly character, he would have opposed such a move.

(4) Finally, at the end of his book, Abbé Godin takes a clear stand against the ideas of the *Jeunesse de l'Eglise*, a movement run by Father Montuclard. In 1950, six years after the death of the abbé, this movement was to have a great influence on the worker-priests when they outlined their own programme: economic and social revolution first, then redemption.

Abbé Godin took the other point of view. 'We do not say "politics-first", or "health-first", or "social-reform-first".

---

[6] The details of this experiment are discussed later in this book.

There must be *at the same time,* sustaining all these efforts, a tremendous surge of youthful and vital Christianity. The world cannot be saved without Christ. Political and social renewal is not Christianity. It can remove obstacles to the progress of faith, but "politics-first" simply leads us into a vicious circle, like an exclusively "spiritual" Christianity. You must have both, each in its place; and the first is specifically the work of the laity. In their enthusiasm for the reconstruction of the worldly city, certain people become too absorbed in manœuvres; the true work of the Church, as Christ taught it and as the apostles realized it, is the deep penetration of Christianity into a large number of souls, who then shine out as witness to the truth in every aspect of their lives.'[7]

Twenty years later, Monsignor Ancel repeated the same idea :

'In their present circumstances, it is extremely difficult for workers to become Christians; that is why there is a serious obligation to work for the betterment of the working-class, and to influence other groups to take account of their needs. *But the evangelization of the working-class cannot wait for these reforms to be completed, and the Church has not sent priests among the proletariat to carry out these reforms. . . .* It is an error to think that evangelization is necessarily linked with social advance, and that the first can only be accomplished via the second. There is an 'economics-first' kind of thinking which is just as false and just as dangerous as the 'politics-first' of *Action Française.*'[8]

DIRECT CONTACT

Within a few weeks of the death of Abbé Godin, several priests of the Mission de Paris obtained permission from the

[7] *France, Pays de Mission,* p. 161.
[8] *Cinq ans avec les Ouvriers.*

archbishop of Paris to go and work in a factory. For the time being, it was only a question of working for limited periods, and Pius XII explicitly approved the authorization —on condition that the cardinal should assume full responsibility for the experiment, and always give it his personal supervision.

What was the object of this factory work? Undoubtedly to know working-class life better—*'pour se désembourgeoiser'*, as the critics mischievously put it. It is true that several priests who came from another *milieu*, and who had been educated in quite a different spirit at their seminaries, resented the need to break out of the categories which kept them apart, and to enter more deeply into the life and soul of the working-class.

Monsignor Ancel described his experiences in this way : 'What struck me most at Gerland was the extent to which I was a *stranger* to the world of the workers, in spite of the fact that I had for so long been concerned with the working-class apostolate. I had been able to talk with Communist workers, and with anarchist workers; I had read books about the economic, social, and political problems which concern the working-class, and I had taken the trouble to acquire a great deal of information; I had even written a number of articles on the working-class and on Communism—studies which, though incomplete, were recognized as having real value. I had, in fact, the reputation of being a priest who knew the world of the workers; but I had to share their lives, as least to a small extent, before I realized how far I was from them. It was then that I understood the difference between what can be learnt at second-hand and from books, and what is learnt day by day in the world of the working-class. It was not the quantity of my knowledge which changed, but its quality'.[9]

[9] op. cit., pp. 107-109.

(a) The working-class training and the priesthood

Rather like Charles de Foucauld at La Trappe, the worker-priests were to discover the difference between 'religious poverty' and the veritable curse of working-class existence : the constant uncertainty about the future, the sordid accommodation and environment, the brutalizing din of the workshops, the physical fatigue so poorly rewarded, and the humiliation of being held of such little account.

To begin with, their spiritual lives, their prayers, and their masses expanded wonderfully through this generosity. It is important not to forget this; even today, the Little Brothers of Jesus live entirely in this environment, so that one cannot maintain that it makes the priestly life impossible. Abbé Michel Favreau, who was killed accidentally at Bordeaux, bears witness to this : 'Prayer', he wrote, 'is much easier for me here than in the turmoil of preparation for meetings and festivities. When you are carrying sacks or boxes, in the crossed shadow of the derricks, it is easy to be united with the passion of Christ. It is Good Friday every day. Moral temptations are much less serious and less tormenting than in the ordinary life of a curate.[10] The great temptation is to become weary of this life—not to belong to it completely, to look for evasions, to fail to realize in one's own life the mystery of the incarnation or the mystery of the cross. My mass has assumed for me a much greater value; and I have also discovered the bible.

There is another painful experience; that is to know that you are misunderstood by practically the entire body of the parochial clergy—to feel as foreign as a real proletarian when you go into a presbytery, or into a church.' We shall come back to this last phrase. Such testimony—and it does not stand alone—demands to be taken seriously.

The evidence of Monsignor Ancel, auxiliary bishop of

[10] Which Abbé Favreau had previously experienced.

26

Lyons and superior-general of Le Prado, who himself lived and worked in the poor district of Gerland for five years, is even more significant:[11] 'I confess that I have learnt more in a spiritual sense during the five years that I spent at Gerland than during the whole of my life as a priest'. (p. 364.)

After quoting certain passages from St. Paul and St. John, he concluded: 'I had studied these texts, and I had meditated about them; but, in the presence of these men without God, I discovered them afresh, with a new richness of meaning'. (p. 367.)

Elsewhere, he gives us an insight into his eucharistic life: 'My stay at Gerland was undoubtedly the occasion of a profound renewal in my celebration of mass'. (p. 435.)

Monsignor Ancel was a disciple of Father Chevrier, the founder of Le Prado; and he said that, since he went to live at Gerland, he had a much better understanding of Father Chevrier's message, and he saw much more clearly its universal application. (p. 23.)

How was this first religious experiment judged by Christians? Here are three typical responses:

'Do we study theology for four or even five years, and receive the holy oil of priesthood, in order to go and shape pieces of metal in a factory or to tighten nuts?'[12]

'As a manual labourer working full-time, a worker-priest earns more than 20,000 francs a month. A priest in a parish would earn far less. Where then is the greater poverty?'[13]

Finally, a letter from a cardinal of the Papal Curia, published in *Aux Ecoutes* (5th February 1954): 'Investigations carried out by order have revealed practices which could be called odious, were they not ridiculous. Some priest

[11] *Cinq ans avec les Ouvriers.*
[12] *La Tribune de Genève, 28th September 1953.*
[13] Jean Madiran in *Rivarol*, 11th February 1954.

27

thinks that he will renew the actions of the Last Supper; so priests in their overalls have a meal with their mates, and then take bread and wine from the table, consecrate them, and give out communion. Elsewhere, the faithful are taught to reply to the liturgical salutation, *Dominus Vobiscum*, with the simple but unexpected mystical formula "O.K." Sometimes we hear of "Comrade Jesus", or "Jesus for the boys—Hip, Hip, Hurrah".'

Anyone who knew the worker-priests, or who has taken part in their meetings or their masses, or lived with them, will be dumbfounded to read such a letter from a Roman cardinal. He did not, of course, invent these tales himself, and one can understand his astonishment and his revulsion; but where on earth did he get them from? When Cardinals Feltin, Liénart, and Gerlier went to Cardinal Ottaviani of the Holy Office with their files on the worker-priests, he replied, 'There's no need to show me them—I have my own'. There is no doubt the denunciations and the slanderous gossip started as early as 1945, long before the worker-priests had begun to take part in political activities.

Even those who disapproved of the worker-priests for a number of reasons usually had the grace to recognize the generosity of their daily sacrifice; but some refused even this amount of justice. The new missionaries were dragged in the mud, calumniated in high places by those right-thinking people who are so assiduous in their attentions to the great. Before we think about the attraction exercised upon them by the Communist Party, it would be as well to think about the scandalous hostility which they met with from their own brothers in the faith.

Certainly there were some strange characters among the worker-priests; are there not in every sphere of the church's life? What of the absent-minded intellectuals among the doctors of the church? What of the odd fellows among the military chaplains, and the maniacs among the parochial clergy? There are 'originals' everywhere. Some of the worker-priests may have abandoned or refused parochial work because they could no longer put up with 'the meanness and pettiness of some aspect of this ministry'; but could this really be called a lack of generosity? A person who was looking for an easy way out would surely find a less exacting 'alibi' than factory work! After all, there are other possibilities. . . .

The texts concerning the spiritual life of these priests are of particular interest.

The first is from Cardinal Pizzardo, at the time of the condemnation on the 24th June 1959: 'On working days it would be almost impossible for a priest to fulfil all the duties of prayer which the church lays upon him—the celebration of daily mass, the recitation of the breviary, mental prayer, a visit to the Blessed Sacrament, and the rosary'.

The worker-priest themselves acknowledged that the concern of the Holy Office on this matter was well founded; it cannot be denied that many of them, because of the heavy social and trade union obligations which were added to their day's work, found themselves neglecting their lives of prayer. But could many priests in the old parish ministry be sure of carrying out all those exercises of piety which Cardinal Pizzardo expects of the worker-priests?

The second quotation is from the worker-priests themselves, during the crisis of 1953-4.

'No doubt we were wrong not to make it clear that our priesthood was contained within our working lives, fashioned by our working lives, and that outside this life we were nothing, not even spiritually. We can no longer accept certain forms of Christianity which are too reminiscent of the *bourgeois* way of life, and which would certainly be rejected by the working-class. This is a challenge to the Church; if one day she hopes to welcome the workers into her family . . . she must find a new way of life, which can be incorporated into this world to which we have married ourselves in faith, and which now conditions even our religious lives'. This may sound astonishing; and yet the words of Father Favreau quoted earlier, and similar testimony from numerous sources, should help us to understand how these priests, like the Little Brothers of Jesus, were able to find in manual work a pattern of spirituality which conditioned their very priesthood. 'Just as a Benedictine or a village priest might lose his footing in the hectic life of a city parish, so a worker-priest could reach a stage when he is no longer able to find his spiritual equilibrium anywhere outside the framework of manual labour.'

The discovery of a new form of priesthood rooted in the conditions of working-class life was of capital importance, and it involved a host of problems which demanded exceptional self-control and generosity. It would already be sufficient to ask a man to keep his balance in such circumstances. But when they became workers these priests were inevitably faced with other discoveries; and the first was that of the working-class world.

(b) The working-class world and the Mission

For many, this expression 'working-class world' is an empty one. Abbé Luc Lefèvre writes in *Pensée Catholique* (No. 28): 'Give me a definition; what is this "Working-class world", this "World of labour"? What substance has it? Let me see it in reality, not in words and ideas. For my part, I can see on our planet only one species of human being, made of flesh and blood, and subject to the law of work. *"Bourgeois"*, "worker", "proletarian", all these are relative terms. And this famous "solidarity" which is supposed to exist among the members of the "working-class world"—isn't this too something in the head rather than a reality?'

Monsignor Ancel's reply is a wise one :

'According to the Marxist theory, the worker is a man apart from others, endowed with virtuous impulses of absolute purity.

'According to the pure humanist theory, the worker is a man just like other men; there is no "working-class soul", there are just men, who happen to work in industry with their hands.

'In fact, when one lives in the working-class world, one is much more inclined to the Marxist view; and those who live outside it, and who are preoccupied with avoiding Marxist contamination, incline the other way.

'During the five years I spent at Gerland, I did indeed see more cars appearing, more household appliances, more television sets; I saw the attitudes of the working-class being modified. But nothing that I saw suggested to me in any way the present or future disappearance of the working-class.'[14]

This is also the view taken by Father Loew, a man no one could accuse of Communist sympathies, who had lived in the working-class environment for twenty years, and was already well-prepared by his university studies to weigh up social realities. This is a summary of what he wrote in his book, *Journal d'une Mission Ouvrière* :[15]

'The security and the very moderate standard of living which he has won, his charter which is the right to work, his world of ideas and his morality, all these come, not from France, but from that labouring class which has gradually raised him, by the efforts of its militants, if not above

[14] *Cinq Ans Avec Les Prêtres-Ouvriers*, pp. 155 and 104.
[15] Editions du Cerf.

poverty, at least above misery, thanks to a fierce and incessant struggle—a struggle which itself has developed culturally, socially, and politically. He owes to the working-class what we owe to France; the working-class is his native land. He is internationalist by instinct. His country has never helped or understood him, as has the working-class in other countries (e.g. the French strike supported by British trade unions). We must understand this feeling, this class-patriotism which cuts across national frontiers, if we are ever to bring the faith in a realistic way to the working-class world.'

The worker-priests discovered a 'world' they had known nothing about. Even those who came from quite humble families did not know the real working-class world, as Father Loew acknowledged:

'Everyone knows that an engineer or a senior official is farther from the working-class mentality than a small local shopkeeper. In reality, it is not a difference in income which is the distinctive note of the working-class, but a whole culture, a whole patrimony of ideas and aspirations.

'My parents were not rich; but I was able to have a secondary education. We belonged to that layer of French society which has the right to inherit the culture of France; France is our country, our true spiritual mother. It is she who has brought us to that spiritual fruition which is beyond price. In common with what one might call the French *bourgeoisie*, we have a fund of culture and of ideas about life and the world which were elaborated by Greco-Roman civilization, and by the centuries of Christianity.

'But we do not find these ideas in the working-class; it is impermeable to them. The artisan, or the small trader, could absorb them without much difficulty; but not the worker.'

Father Perrin had long before felt a foreigner amongst the French workers drafted to Germany; in France, the worker-priests felt the same sense of exile. They realized that a profound adaptation was needed if they were to take root in this new and surprising world. They were soon convinced that it was impossible to evangelize it from outside, and they understood why the Y.C.W. and the parishes had failed by remaining 'outside'.

The Church, they felt, simply was not there, in this world which had been formed outside her during the preceding century. Because there was no exchange between them, the two worlds were unable to understand each other, and were even unaware of each other's existence.

Abbé Favreau, whom we quoted earlier, wrote : 'In the church I visited yesterday evening, to see the priest, there were about a dozen old people reciting the rosary (it was six o'clock). What a painful contrast with the travelling fair a hundred and fifty yards away, and the lively activity in the streets. We are carefully guarding the dead cinders, without seeing that others have burst into flames.

'It is not that I am against the rosary . . . but what are we to think of a church of the aged . . . a small handful of religious bigots. I cannot say mass in a parish, because of the "scandal" of a mass said in the evening by a fellow in civilian clothes—a fellow, incidentally, who is increasingly grimy and black with oil. The priest however took me to a religious house, and they welcomed me with open arms.'

Such discoveries were a shock to the worker-priests; it was almost as if they had to change their nationality. They had to develop a new mentality, create in themselves a new set of responses. In addition, to these personal difficulties, they had to face a further trial; the *bourgeois*-Christian *milieu*, from which they had set out, became for them as a foreign land. Their loneliness was appalling.

'The eyes of these priests, who were, so to speak, "incarnate" in the world, were progressively dimmed, and when they looked at the Church of God, they did not realize that they saw it with proletarian eyes. The intervention of the Church was like a painful but salutary surgical operation; a less substantial reform would not have been sufficient."[16]

Missionaries who set out for foreign lands are supported by an immense movement of sympathy, prayer, and material aid; the worker-priests, on the other hand, struggling in their mission against overwhelming difficulties, were soon to be the butt of criticism from their own brothers in the faith.

When they were burdened with this problem of finding their spiritual equilibrium as priests in the working-class, and of striking roots in this unknown territory, amidst distrust, slander, and irony, they were faced with a new and crucial challenge; that of the trade union movement.

(c) The Christian virtues and the soul of the working-class

Father Loew observes that 'The working-class world is not a "perfect society". On the contrary, it is a society which is continuously reaching out towards a goal which it has not yet reached; and on this depends its structures, its mentality, its ideas.

'The "mystique" of the working-class has simple origins; it is born of hardship, and of the need to escape from it. It is not just a dream; the worker believes in reality, and in the realizable. The vision only took shape in the course of action, as the working-class became conscious that it possessed both the power and the organization to realize its purposes.'

This touches on two aspects of the working-class which distinguish it from the *bourgeoisie* :

First, its *dynamic* vision of the world, as constantly evolving, searching, progressing—the very contrary of con-

[16] *Documentation Catholique,* 21st May 1954.

34

formism, traditionalism, and the eternal reference to the past. Christianity also is essentially dynamic; but it is only too often frozen into static clerical forms.

Secondly, its realism; the working-class is suspicious of ideas; it does not understand them well enough to know where they are leading to. It prefers palpable facts; that is why it demands of the Christian apostle, not an intellectual sermon, but a real involvement, a living sacrifice, something which is authentic and verifiable.

For another reason too the worker is distrustful of ideas. His hardship demands not theories, but acts of liberation. As his suffering is concrete, so must his liberation be concrete. The worker-priests soon found that they could not dissipate the distrust of the Church without action, involvement, and risk.

What does the working-class want? Father Loew has his own answer : 'Born in constraint and servitude, the working-class is carried upwards by a positive aspiration to a new and better order, to what the Pope called recently "a world of justice and of brotherhood". The worker believes there is injustice in the sharing-out of profit; he wishes to exercise control over this, and to stand up against the injustice. . . . He wants a new world in which the worker will have a say in the way his work is used, and in the way its fruits are distributed. This aspiration is not to be understood as simply a part of the Marxist dialectic.

'The worker is not anti-hierarchy—he is too much of a realist for that, too much aware of the need for organization; but with all his heart he is anti-privilege. He sees injustice parading the factory-floor in the person of the boss's son, perhaps poorly gifted, who will step into his father's shoes without effort, while his own boy will have difficulty in qualifying as a skilled workman. One of the main demands of the worker is that everyone should start life on an equal footing, and have an equal opportunity to bring to fruition the gifts of nature.'

The worker-priests wondered how these demands could be contrary to the gospels or to the natural law, and were astonished that they were not pressed more frequently, more courageously, and more realistically in the Christian world, with its 'hunger and thirst for justice'. It seemed to them that their new priesthood was more authentic, more scriptural, than anything which they had left behind. They felt that in their previous lives there had been a great deal of ignorance, a great deal of cowardice—even a betrayal of Christ, and of their brothers, the poor. . . . Living themselves in the working-class environment, they saw that there was a whole world standing in opposition to their just demands, and that progress could come only through conflict: 'For a Marxist, that sounds like part of the system; for the worker, it is simply an observation of fact. The boss does not give anything away unless he has to.

'The working-class, like us, has its ideas about the world; ideas born, as ours once were, from strife, and now fundamental to its way of life'.

If the Church teaches 'not *revolution* but *evolution*', the working-class, speaking from the world of social realities, replies that this is impossible. The worker-priest, living among them, concludes that the Church's views are pure theory, and that Marxism alone matches up to the real world.

Father Loew, however, was convinced that Marxism had frozen, and even restricted, this vision which is always present in the heart of the working-class. . . . 'Marxism seems to me a materialized, hardened, and narrow expression of the living aspirations of the workers. A worker will often express his ideas in Communist terms; but the discussion and the action which follow show that his soul aspires beyond this

36

conceptualization. The Christian apostle must understand this'.

These are the words of a man well-grounded in law and political science, with more than fifteen years experience of the life which he is describing. The worker-priests had neither this experience nor this training to enable them to make a critical examination of the realities which faced them.

They were soon, however, to discover the specific virtues of the working-class: their solidarity, frankness, and their sincerity. This sincerity is not just an intellectual virtue, it is the quality of a man who acts according to his conscience, his principles, his ideals. To be 'frank' is to be without affectation; you laugh when you feel like laughing, and if there is something wrong you say so. The militants are rough and speak roughly—but they get equally rough replies, and they do not resent them. They are not, like us, 'polite' and 'diplomatic'.

The worker-priest, then, found himself in a world in some ways surprisingly close to the mind of Christ:

(a) by its very real poverty;

(b) by its just aspirations;

(c) by certain virtues which are of the essence of Christianity, and which Christ named as the distinctive characteristics of His Church: its solidarity (which is charity), and its simplicity (see Matt. xviii).[17]

Of course, these working-class virtues are certainly not the perfection of the Christian ideal; but many 'Christians' fall very far short of them in comparison with the 'atheistic' workers!

There was a further discovery to be made: 'These virtues are not just the flotsam left over from the shipwreck of the

[17] The word 'solidarity' which may seem rather flat to us meant for the worker-priests a life of the greatest devotion, generosity, and self-sacrifice—in fact it meant nothing more or less than greatness of soul.

catechism, nor are they a family heritage which can be traced back to Christian ancestors. They are the virtues formed by trade unionism, by the living example of working-class militants; and it is these militants who possess them in a more vital and active form than their fellows. Many other dominant ideas come from the working-class movement, from the experiences and lessons of former strife rather than from theory or doctrine; the dynamic ideal of the new world of justice and brotherhood, the passionate love of the working-class, the idea that war is of no concern to the worker, who is merely a tool in it, the complete absence of national prejudice, the sense of international solidarity, etc. etc. These ideas are the common property of the working-class, deeper than Marxism, Communism, or anarchism.

'The militants are the privileged personalities of the working-class world. They are to be found everywhere, and they give to this society its own peculiar structure. They are the people who express what the others can only feel, who translate the confused aspirations into clear ideas, who can train men to effective action, bringing into play the passions, the virtues, and sometimes the vices, which they know so well. They do not always, as is commonly thought, appeal to self-interest. They are implicitly recognized as leaders, or rather as teachers. The mass recognizes itself in them; theirs is the responsibility for training the minds and directing the actions of their colleagues.'

The labour movement for more than a century has been slowly working out a fund of ideas and beliefs common to the working-class, and has at the same time provided the masses with their finest example of moral virtue. It is the labour movement which has continually thrown up the heroes of the working-class, men of action and initiative as well as moral greatness, living models for their fellows. They do not exactly *create* public opinion; but public opinion cannot take shape without them.

'The evangelization of the working-class is the evangelisation of a structured society, which must be seen as a dynamic and living whole; to treat it as a mere collection of individuals would be to court frustration and failure.'

It is easy to understand therefore why these militants exercised a powerful influence on the worker-priests themselves; for they too saw in the words and leadership of these men the clear expression of all that they felt in a confused form.

They were such novices! Some beginner worker-priests showed the typical novices' awkwardness, feeling that they *had* to dress badly, even on Sundays, to talk in a kind of coarse language that even workers did not use all the time, etc. It is not hard to understand how the more advanced worker-priests felt the temptation to take positions of greater responsibility in the labour movement. They were in fact offered such positions. A political manœuvre, maybe; but this facile explanation should not be used to conceal the profound problems which were involved. It is often said that the worker-priests were not prepared for their task; but did the church know—does she still know—what is really involved in this task?

A last tragic discovery: 'What strikes a priest as soon as he makes the effort to have continuous contact with the working-class is the gulf between the Church and the working-class. The Church is considered hostile to the working-class and to its aspirations, favouring capitalism and the subordination of the workers. It's no use quoting encyclicals against this universal conviction, for it is a judgement of fact . . . Christians do not take part in the demonstrations of the workers, the workers do not take part in the demonstrations of Christians.'

Faced with this situation, the worker-priests felt 'that vague hostile presentiment one has when facing an unknown world which is supposed to be charged with hatred.'[18]

All the problems were heaped on the worker-priest at once; they had no preparatory experience, no training. It was too much for a small handful of men, who had to face at the same time the lack of understanding, the distrust, and the open or insidious attacks of their fellow Christians and of their fellow priests.

[18] In the book from which we have already quoted, Monsignor Ancel repeats a number of the ideas of Father Loew; at the same time he enriches them by his own fascinating study of the working-class vocabulary, the development of working-class thought, and the influences which affect the working-class world (see pp. 107-235).

CHAPTER II

The Choice

THE ACTIVITIES of the worker-priests soon diverged both from the ideas of Abbé Godin, and from the directives laid down by Cardinal Suhard on the 14th January 1944, when he stated: 'The direct aim of the mission is to convert pagans; its indirect aim is to show the Christian community that it must change its own attitudes. We have to blaze a new trail; much has been achieved during the past fifteen years by Catholic Action, but now the mission must go further.'

What was demanded of the worker-priests was a double loyalty: they had to be both genuine workers, and genuine apostles. As Father Chaillet put it in *Témoignage Chrétien*, they had to 'combine an authentic working-class life with a no less authentic fidelity to the missionary spirit of the Church, and to the exigencies of the priestly life.'

The temporal choice

This double loyalty was not easy to achieve. Cardinal Montini had said that 'a good, true, human and holy priesthood could save the world'; but how exactly is a priest, placed amidst the sufferings and struggles of the working-class, to be 'good, true, human and holy'? Father Dillard, a worker-priest in Germany, said that it was essential to break the barriers which separated the priest from his fellows. How was this to be done?

41

If men claim just rights, which they are unable to obtain without struggling for them, can a man be really a priest for these men without taking part in their struggle? The workers distrust ideas; they believe in acts. Many worker-priests decided that they *had* to take part in this struggle, and that they could only do so effectively through trade unions. 'The unions', wrote Abbé Daniel, 'are working for greater justice in industry.'

We shall look at the arguments used for and against this involvement:

Arguments in favour

'The people are hungry for bread, and for justice. The working-class family wants a roof over its head, and work to ensure its subsistence. Rummage-sales and charity fairs are not enough; nor is the devotion of an Abbé Pierre. The worker-priests realized that life is a continuous struggle of the exploited against the exploiters.' (Mohammed el Hadj; *L'Algérie Libre*, 5th March 1954).

'Through the worker-priests, the Church is present in the working-class world. They do not want only to talk about justice; they want to work for justice, in the name of Christ. It is this work which they are being asked to abandon'. (A young priest in *Express*, 12th February 1954.)

'If, knowing that men are in need of bread, we have no desire to satisfy their hunger, we are pretending to despise the very thing we ask for every day in our prayers, and we forget that Jesus called Himself the Bread of Life. It is hard to explain the consecration of bread to someone who is short of daily bread, when you are taking no steps to satisfy his need.' (A. Béguin, *Esprit*, March 1954.)

'These commitments are justified by human need; they are no more surprising than the political and military commitments in former times of the bishops who were *defensores civitatis* (defenders of the city).' (Editorial *Actualité Religieuse*, 15th September 1954.)

'If certain priests caused surprise and scandal by taking up political and trade union posts, it was because they thought there was a remedy for the misery which surrounded them—but a remedy demanding courageous action in terms of collective justice, rather than acts of individual charity.' (Georges Hourdin.)

Arguments against

'Jesus Christ often told the rich to give their goods to the poor; but He never invited the poor to take them for themselves.' (R. Johannet, *Rivarol*, 26th February 1954.)

'By an amazing piece of spiritual trickery, a number of our contemporaries have been brought to believe that a worldly paradise is possible. Even Christians sometimes share this extraordinary belief, which is surely the greatest of all lies. Christianity has good reason to steer clear of such an error.' (*France Catholique*, 13th November 1953.)

'Christ in His charity shares with everyone the sufferings which he endures; but He does not share with everyone His fight against injustice. . . . It is not for Christ's messengers always to be concerned with other people's crimes. Christ did not come to save the just; and if the working-class is indeed an innocent victim, one would not expect to find Christ there.' (Jean Madiran, *Rivarol*, 11th February 1954.)

'There is a world from which we must stand aloof, a world in which one must not be "present" without reserve. That world is the "mystery of iniquity", the organized power of the Prince of this world. How can the world which develops outside the Church be salutary for humanity? And to what extent can Christians be bound to it?' (Abbé Richard, *L'Homme Nouveau*, 1st November 1953.)

'Why so much talk of the "disaffected masses?" The masses are always the masses. . . . What counts is rather the *élite*, whose influence is based on its fidelity to immutable principles.' (*L'Echo de Bigorre*, Pierre L'Hermite, 6th February 1954.)

Here are the *Conclusions of the Worker-Priests*, taken from their *Document Vert* of the 3rd November 1954 : 'We do not consider that our lives as workers have ever prevented us from remaining loyal to our faith and our priesthood. We find it impossible to understand how, in the name of the gospel, priests can be forbidden to share the conditions of millions of oppressed human beings, and to join in their struggles. Of course the worker-priests, by their activities and even by their very existence, disturbed the consciences of those who were in the habit of using religion to serve their own prejudices and class-interests; the pressures exerted by such people, and denunciations from numerous sources, help to account for the steps which are now being taken.'

Why should so many of the worker-priests have chosen the C.G.T.—a Communist trade union? The answer is given in *Réforme* (13th February 1954): 'The worker-priests judged that the Church was too closely bound up with the interests of one class; and they were drawn into a struggle which seemed to correspond more closely with a Marxist than with a Christian scheme of the world'. The article goes on, 'It was not "temporal commitments" they were being asked to renounce; it was commitment to the working-class'.

Father Andrew differed from this last opinion : 'The complaint is not just that the worker-priests have taken up positions in political and trade union movements, but that they have taken up political attitudes closely allied to those of the Communist Party, and adopted trade union policies modelled on those of the C.G.T. (*Grandeurs et Erreurs des Prêtres-Ouvriers* : p. 134.)

44

Two factors influenced certain worker-priests to join the
C.G.T.

First, they had no confidence in the Christian organizations. They were afraid of half-measures, and suspected that
clerical influences worked in favour of the employers or of
capitalism, in a way that amounted to a betrayal of the
working-class. They sensed in the Christian attitude to the
working-class timidity and betrayal; that is why they not
only refused to join the C.F.T.C., but were generally suspicious of the Christians who did join. They refused to
collaborate with them, and considered them to be strangers
to, if not enemies of, the working-class.

Secondly, they joined the C.G.T. because they believed
that *the Communist Party was the only authentic representative of the cause of the workers,* the only one which had
the courage to follow its principles to their conclusions, the
only one which stood up for economic justice and the
interests of the whole community. In this they shared a
working-class response which was part of the world of fact,
rather than the world of theory and ideas.

How did they come to adopt this attitude? Through the
experience of strikes? through a comparison of the aims of
the C.F.T.C. with those of the C.G.T. during the years
1945-9? Did they really see this timidity in action, this
betrayal in the very statement of problems?

It is important to remember that just after the liberation,
the winds of social revolution were blowing strongly in
France; they soon died down in the upper classes, but among
the masses the great hope lasted longer. During this period,
the Communists were intensely active—both by direct
propaganda, which could have influenced some worker-
priests, and also by indirect propaganda, as for instance
through the Peace Movement, which all men of goodwill
were invited to join, for a cause in itself eminently just.

What influenced the priests far more strongly, however, was a kind of synthesis between Marxism and Christianity which was at that time being sketched out by 'progressive' Christian thinkers.

The religious choice

The worker-priests themselves put the problem in this way: 'We are deeply impressed by the unaccustomed problems we have had to face, and by the superficial and mechanical way in which traditionally minded Christians talk about poverty, de-Christianization, spirituality, evangelization. The positions we took up, and for which we are attacked, are inescapable, even if they do present serious problems.'[1]

They are quite conscious that their attitude is somewhat abnormal; but they are firmly convinced that there is no other solution. It is this dilemma we have to understand.

In the spring of 1947, some Catholic Communists and Communist sympathisers founded the U.C.P. (Union of Christian Progressives.) Immediately, E. M. Mounier wrote in *Esprit* (July 1947): 'It is impossible to have a double loyalty—to the Communist Party, for the problems of the world; and to Christianity, for the problems of heaven.'

During the strikes of November-December 1947, the U.C.P. supported the C.G.T. as the only union which was effectively fighting capitalism. In the manifesto published at the time, it stated that the Communist Party is today the only means of defending the working-class, and the only hope for establishing in the future a popular democracy.

In June 1948, Mounier published a special edition of *Esprit* devoted entirely to the question of Marxism. Two

[1] National meeting of worker-priests held at Lyons, 15th and 16th December 1951.

articles were of particular interest to theologians; one was on God, and the other on matter. In these articles, Fathers Desroches and Chenu abandoned all *a priori* opposition to Marxism, and tried to enter into dialogue with it.

Why, asked Father Desroches, does Marxism call itself 'atheistic'? Marxist arguments, properly speaking, do not impinge either on God or on the Bible. What is it, then, that is being rejected? It is *false representations of God*, which Christians often idolize, either through ignorance, or conformism, or through self-interest. . . . Let everyone consider for himself the gulf which separates his own religious life from the spirit of the gospels, and he will soon realize why it is that people find it hard to form any clear idea of God or of His revelation through the witness of our lives.

Would not a dialogue with Marxism be profitable to both sides? Through it, perhaps, Marxism might discover God; and Christians might clarify their theology, and learn to bring their lives more into line with their principles.

Father Chenu, for his part, regrets that a certain kind of scholastic philosophy seems to be content with defining matter, which is inferior to spirit. He is convinced that a dialogue with Marxism could be for the Christian an occasion for great theological enrichment, and thinks that a positive philosophy of matter, exploring quite new domains of thought, could result from it.

These two articles provoked many reactions. The 'integralists' were clearly in opposition, such as Father Fessard (*Etudes*, January 1949), who expressed fears that these theologians would push young Catholics into the perilous adventure of progressivism; he queried the timing rather than the thesis of the articles. Monsignor Ancel, on the other hand, denounced the errors of Christian progressivism; 'Christians', he wrote, 'are deceiving themselves if they think they can collaborate habitually with the Communist Party and yet keep their minds independent of Marxism . . . it is a mistake to imagine that you can remain in agreement and still remain independent . . . anyone who habitually collaborates with the Communist Party falls increasingly under the influence of Marx, and, without even being aware of it, inclines towards atheistic materialism'. (*Témoignage Chrétien*, 15th July 1949.)

A year later, Monsignor Ancel wrote : 'Anyone who submits to Marxist influence is by that very fact, as Lenin foresaw, in danger of losing his faith. . . . Gradually, the moral conscience is modified from within, and calculates more and more in terms of expediency. . . . Gradually, all other considerations are obscured by the sole concern for worldly justice. Christianity is accepted only when it helps to establish this justice, and rejected when it is first of all directed towards God. Next it is accused of being a religion irrelevant to life; it is sharply criticized, and the attacks of its enemies are readily accepted. Criticism of Communism provokes a hypersensitive response, in the name of "charity"; but criticism of bishops is credulously accepted—in the name of "truth".' (*Témoignage Chrétien*, 9th June 1950.)

The Progressives, consistently with their beliefs, worked for the C.G.T. and rallied to the Communist-inspired movements, such as the Peace Partisans.

It should not be assumed, however, that all who joined this movement were 'progressivists'. A number of the worker-priests were; and a number were sympathetic. Others, on the other hand, were very unsympathetic. Bernanos, in his *Dialogue des Carmélites*, puts a much neglected truth into the mouth of the mother-superior, a woman of sound common-sense : 'You can never really say "the community wants this" or "the community wants that"; the community has no common will; in all human groups, there are the weak and the strong, the ones who are for and the ones who are against'. It is only just to recognize that this also applies to the worker-priests.

The real progressivism which was condemned, is described by Monsignor Ancel: it says, in effect, 'The rise of the working-class is one of the major evolutionary developments of the twentieth century, and Communism is the sole motive force of this movement. The Christian must therefore collaborate with Communism.' The common device of 'integralists', for their part, is to label as 'progressivist' any progressive move of which they happen to disapprove.

In this period of crisis, we have no right to waste our time on this sterile and partisan debate, which is, in any case, the rightful concern of the psychoanalyst rather than of the Christian thinker.

Calendar of Events[2]

1944 : The first priests started work, with the consent of Cardinal Suhard and the approval of the Pope. They started by working for temporary periods, but they were soon taking permanent positions.

1945 : On the 9th April Abbé Folliet was wounded in the head while he was in the Alps, and died at the age of 37. He was a priest who had been deported by the Italian police during the war, and after the liberation had been attached to the Mission de Paris, working at B.M.W. in Argenteuil.

The Bishop of Annecy officiated at the funeral, and preached the funeral sermon. In the choir of the Church were the flags of many organizations—Action Catholique, Scouts de France, Anciens Combatants, C.G.T., the Com-

---

[2] A number of the events here recorded are commented on in *Grandeurs et Erreurs des Prêtres-Ouvriers* (Amiot-Dumont, 1955), and in *Les Prêtres-Ouvriers* (Editions de Minuit—anonymous), according to the differing viewpoints of their authors.

munist Party, and the S.F.I.O. On the 3rd November 1945, *La Croix* wrote : 'Abbé Folliet's holy audacity should teach us that at this critical time Christians must be free to act and to commit themselves'.

20th June : For the first time the Vatican, relying on information 'worthy of belief', expressed to Cardinal Suhard serious concern about the worker-priests. Slanderous reports and anonymous letters began to reach the Archbishop of Paris. Up to that time, no political position had been taken by the worker-priests.

11th-13th July : Cardinal Suhard was present at a study week-end, which defined anew the aims of the Mission : 'To bring the Church to birth in the bosom of the proletariat, considered as a body of people with its own peculiar mentality, its own way of life, and its own organization'.

1946-7; October : Two priests belonging to the C.T.G. defined their purpose in the following terms : 'The aim of the Mission is to participate with all our strength in the human and spiritual liberation of the proletariat'. (*Human* was the new word.) 'We wish to identify ourselves with the forces which represent the working-class and we shall maintain this identification so long as it does not conflict directly with our Christian conscience, or with the true solidarity of all wage-earners'. ('Conditional' adherence.)

20th November : Cardinal Suhard gave his instructions to Father Hollande, the Superior of the Mission, before his journey to Rome : 'It is high time you went', he observed. Denunciations were pouring into the Vatican from France.

29th November : Father Hollande was received by Cardinal Ottaviani; he submitted a report, sought authorization for the worker-priests to celebrate mass in the evenings, and asked also for a relaxation of the fasting rules. The account which he gave of the situation in France, and of the means necessary to remedy it, were perfectly understood, and the attitude of the Pope especially was encouraging. Father Hollande felt that Rome would like the bishops concerned to submit detailed reports of the exact situation in their dioceses, and thought that the authorization he sought would be granted. One of the ecclesiastical dignitaries who worked directly with the Pope said, 'When so much is at stake, risks must be taken, in case one should be guilty of failing to do all that is possible for the salvation of the world'.

1947; 18th January: Encouraged by this sympathetic reception, Cardinal Suhard sent Father Hollande back to Rome for a second visit; but this time he found a much more tense situation.

11th February: Cardinal Suhard published his great pastoral letter, *Essor ou Déclin de l'Eglise*. It was translated throughout the Catholic world. Some people criticized the cardinal for having exerted an influence 'greater than that of the Pope in his encyclicals'.

15th February: Cardinal Suhard sent to the Holy Office a report answering the queries this body had put concerning the worker-priests. Did they fulfil the obligations of the priesthood? Was evening mass really necessary? Why this new form of apostolate? Did it not harm the traditional ministry of the priest? Were there not other ways of penetrating the masses?

First months of 1947: Foundation of the Union of Christian Progressives (U.C.P.).

November to December: A great wave of strikes, in which worker-priests took part. Cardinal Suhard expressed approval of the strikes.

Certain employers, disappointed by the attitude of the priests, who they had hoped would lead the workers back to 'the path of duty', asked the bishops to recall them. In well-informed ecclesiastical circles it soon began to be

51

rumoured that the worker-priest venture was drawing to a close.

1948; November: The first National Assembly of the *Movement for Liberty and Peace*, founded in August at Breslau, in Poland, during a peace congress of intellectuals. The movement was Communist inspired, but was addressed to the entire world. The closing address was given on the 28th of November by Abbé Boulier, a priest who had worked with the Jesuits of Action Populaire at Vanves, had then been a curate at Plaisance, and, after the liberation of Paris, parish-priest at St. Dévote in Monaco. During his address he said, 'If we, who are struggling for peace, are asked, "Who are the Communists among us?" we shall reply, "All of us!"' Many worker-priests and other churchmen in France supported the Peace Movement, which was a popular movement of opposition to the Western military and economic alliance.

5th December: Cardinal Suhard celebrated the fiftieth year of his priesthood in Notre-Dame. He spoke of his attachment to the Mission de Paris, and pronounced these memorable words: 'The first task is to save the souls of the people of Paris; it is for these masses that I shall have to answer on the Day of Judgement. This is the thought which weighs on me day and night. When I see these crowds, my heart is wrung. I am constantly meditating about how to break down the barrier which separates the Church from the masses—for unless it is broken down Christ cannot be given back to the people who have lost Him. That is why we have entrusted the Mission de Paris to specially chosen priests, who are in the forefront of the Church's advance'.

1949; 5th February: Three months before his death, and a few days before the condemnation of the Italian progressives, Cardinal Suhard warned Catholics in a solemn message against 'habitual and close collaboration with Communism'.

5th March: The following cautious commentary on the cardinal's message was published in *L'Osservatore Romano*: 'It is not just a "habitual and close" collaboration which is to be avoided. The greatest vigilance is needed, even in small actions where there is any risk of error'. This is reminiscent of the final absolute condemnation of Communism by Pius XI (March 1937): "Communism is intrinsically perverse, and no collaboration with it can be allowed on any ground. . . .' Jean Verlhac soon gave his reply: 'The militant worker who has committed himself with the Communists, who is seeking for more humane conditions of work for his fellows, who is striving in the face of all manner of opposition to build houses for those who need them, is now to be denied the sacraments; but the industrial magnate who underpays his workers, the big-business-man who throttles his competitors, will still approach the Holy Table without a qualm to receive the Body of Christ'.

31st March: *L'Osservatore Romano* payed homage to the Mission de Paris and to Cardinal Suhard, who, it said, had 'warmly assumed full responsibility for it'. The article concluded, 'One day greater hatred will be directed against them than against other workers; since they are better than their comrades, are they not also—more dangerous? But only one thing is necessary for these men, who are seeking God in poverty, for themselves and for others; and that is to know that they are following in the footsteps of Christ, the Lord of the humble.'

7th May: The worker-priests held their first national meeting. Now that they shared the conditions of the workers, they no longer saw social injustice as amateurs see it, or as sociologists see it, from the outside; they had crossed the barrier. There were an increasing number of calls on their time, and they were obliged to attend more and more meetings; there was a danger of sacrificing the minimum time set aside for their spiritual lives.

Knowing from experience how the material conditions of the worker hindered evangelization and stifled the inner life, they were inclined to think it essential to start with economic and social liberation. They realized, on the other hand, that they were not in any way prepared for such a task, and that their secular and religious education gave them no answer to their difficulties. They were cut off from the Christian community, had little contact with the hierarchy (apart from Cardinal Suhard), and were unjustly suspected and denounced by unthinking Catholics. They decided to hold an annual national assembly; this was the only positive result of their meeting, apart from the sharing of common sorrows and difficulties.

At about the same time, Cardinal Suhard said to Monsignor Ancel, 'Of course I do not approve of all that they do; but it's like gardening—you must take your time. To begin with, it's all a tangle; you don't know which branches to cut back, and which to leave.'

Basically, what the cardinal hoped for was that they would find their balance and progress in holiness, until after four or five years of ministry they would constitute a vigorous *élite* able to accede to the highest positions in the diocese. Formerly he had permitted them to omit the breviary; now, he asked them to say part of it. Some of them said that this was impossible, and the cardinal regretted it.

30th May: Cardinal Suhard died, after giving his last blessing to the Mission and to France. His last words were: 'Not one of these little ones must perish'. (Matt. xviii. 14.)

Only a month and a half before his death he had written in his last pastoral, *Prêtre dans la Cité*: 'The Christianization of this new world calls for a complete intellectual renewal; it will perhaps be a long time before we are able to outgrow the methods of medieval Christianity'.

28th June: The Holy Office excommunicated all those who 'knowingly and with full consent defended the materialistic doctrines of Communism'. Two days afterwards, the Pope gave his approval to this decree. It expressly affected those who joined the Communist Party, those who printed or distributed Communist literature, and those who collaborated or who read this literature. *L'Osservatore Romano* made it clear that the decree did not affect those Catholics who, misled by the promises of the Communist leaders and feeling the urgency of social reform, favoured the Communist Party without adopting its fundamental doctrines. On the other hand, it *did* affect all those organizations directed by Communists. The progressivists and the members of the C.G.T. did not consider that they were affected by 'the letter' of the decree of excommunication.

Four French cardinals commented in turn on the decree of the Holy Office: 'To put ones reputation or ones literary talent at the service of Communism, even if only to write or speak about literature, music, or sport, would be to compromise oneself dangerously by favouring the tactics of a party which specializes in mental seduction. By condemning the action of Communist parties, the Church is not taking the side of capitalism; on the contrary, in the very idea of capitalism there is a kind of materialism which is rejected by Christian teaching. . . . We are well aware of the grief that will be caused to workers by this condemnation of Communism. We know that they see above all in the Communist Party a resolute champion against the social injustice from which they suffer, struggling to give them their rightful place as free men in their work and in their country. We are moved by their sorrow, and we wish to remove the painful impression that the Church is unsympathetic to their aspirations. On the contrary, both before and after the decree, the Church has been unmistakably on their side in the social struggle. For more than fifty years the Popes have taught incessantly that the condition of workers in the present régime is contrary to the demands of justice.'

This decree sent the journalists swarming after the worker-priests to have their comments and declarations. Father Hollande refused to make any statement: 'The worker-priests', he said, 'do not need publicity'.

July: At the very moment when the decree appeared, the conflict between the Vatican and the Czechoslovakian Government reached its climax; in June a schismatic branch of *Action Catholique* was formed, and Abbé Boulier spoke at Velherad on the same platform as Abbé Plohjar, an excommunicated priest who was an active agent of the National Church. A few days later, Monsignor Beaussard, capitulary vicar of Paris, declared that, as from 14th September, Abbé Boulier would no longer be able to celebrate mass. On his return to Paris, Abbé Boulier went to see Monsignor Beaussard, and promised to remain silent and faithful to his ministry; the censure was therefore removed. Abbé Boulier recommenced his collaboration with *Action*, in co-operation with the Peace Partisans.

2nd October: In all the great cities of Europe, meetings were held to condemn President Truman, American imperialism, and its 'European agents'; three weeks afterwards a fortnight's protest against the atomic bomb was organized, which was to last just under a year.

19th November: A worker-priest who was employed in a laundry was dismissed by his employer because 'he did not want priests around the place'. The priest sued him for breach of contract and won his case.

1950; March: The Peace Movement held a plenary

session in Stockholm, and launched a series of 'petitions'. Among the signatories were Monsignor Chevrot, Jean Lacroix, Father Peret, etc. . . . . The priests of Limoges were disowned by their bishop for taking part in such a demonstration.

July: The Holy Office received a note from Father Hollande of the Mission de Paris, expressing his desire that novelty-seekers, mischief-makers, and all unstable characters should be excluded from the apostolate of the worker-priests.

15th September: Pius XII declared in a radio message on the occasion of the international congress of the Y.C.W.: 'Even Catholics sometimes make the common error of classifying human souls; there are not, in fact, two kinds of men—the "workers", and "non-workers" '.

23rd September: Pius XII put the clergy on their guard against 'the spirit of innovation'.

26th November: Cardinal Piazza expressed fears that 'the spirit of the Church is being undermined by dangerous contacts'.

1951; 4th February: Abbé Henri Barreau, who had belonged to the Mission de Paris since his return from captivity, was elected secretary of the Seine division of the Union of Metalworkers—a very important post, since the metalworkers are one of the most militant groups of the Paris proletariat. Abbé Daniel explained to the archbishop that there was no difference between being a member of a trade union and having a full-time trade union post. The archbishop accepted this explanation.

10th February: At a national meeting of worker-priests, Monsignor Ancel read a letter from Cardinal Ottaviani. The cardinal questioned: (1) whether the priests had enough time to pray, (2) whether they were able to maintain the ecclesiastical virtues, (3) whether their generosity might not be better employed in the traditional apostolate. (The same queries that he had raised on 15th February, 1947.)

7th April: The worker-priests had their first martyr: Michel Favreau, a dock-labourer at Marseilles, was crushed to death by the collapse of a pile of timber.

9th June: Cardinal Gerlier was received by the Pope, who expressed his continued confidence in the French episcopate.

20th June: The Holy See judged that the apostolate of the worker-priests was 'more dangerous than it was useful'. It demanded that the existing number of worker-priests should not be exceeded (there were then eighty-five), and that those who had attached themselves to the movement without canonical permission should be recalled. The Holy Office asked for a personal record of every worker-priest, and an annual report of his activities.

End of 1951: The movement *Jeunesse de L'Eglise* was rapidly extending its influence.

1952; 14th January: In agreement with the management of a Lyons factory, at which a worker-priest had for five years been an active member of the C.G.T., a member of a religious order was taken on as an employee, with the purpose of instilling into the other workers a distrust of the worker-priest, and of questioning his trade union allegiance. This manœuvre called forth a united protest from all worker-priests.

16th-17th February: A further national meeting of the worker-priests was held at Lyons; they considered sadly the criticism which had reached their ears: 'You are workmen, but not priests; as priests you are no longer of any use'.

2nd March: Monsignor Harscouet, Bishop of Chartres, attacked the worker-priests in his Lenten pastoral, and repudiated 'the search for a new civilization'.

At the same time a novel by Cesbron was published

called *Les Saints vont en Enfer*. The worker-priests were not pleased with the book. Father Depierre saw in it, quite rightly, a romantic version of his own life at Montreuil, in which truth and fantasy were dangerously mixed. Others found that the book did echo their state of mind as it had been in 1948, but not as it was in 1952.

11th March: On the occasion of a meeting of the bishops and cardinals of France, and after consultation with the worker-priests, the bishops who had these workers in their dioceses issued a joint instruction: They repeated a number of points which had previously been elaborated, the earliest in April 1951, in an attempt to control the movement by directives. These were: insistence on a regular life of prayer, on submission to the bishops, on positive evangelization, on communion with the working-class without temporal commitment. The first formulations had been strongly criticized at the time by the worker-priests, and Monsignor Ancel had been responsible for long negotiations over them in September 1951. Previous to this, the bishops had agreed, as the worker-priests asked of them, 'not to discuss but to listen'.

30th March: Cardinal Feltin made a vigorous attack in his Lenten pastoral on the denunciatory methods employed by the integralists. At this time, the police were carrying out inquiries about the worker-priests and compiling reports on their activities. One worker-priest had addressed a great peace assembly of 12,000 at Limoges; on the previous day, the police had tried in vain to get the bishop to prevent this.

2nd May: The worker-priests protested against the choice of Barcelona for the International Eucharistic Congress; they called it 'a martyred and symbolic city, where militant workers awaited death in prison cells for breaking the conspiracy of silence which surrounds the suffering of the people'.

28th May: The Peace Movement, in defiance of police prohibition, held a meeting of protest against General Ridgeway, then on his way to Paris. Two worker-priests (Louis Bouyer, who was working at Hispano-Suiza, and Bernard Cagne, working at Simca), were arrested and beaten up by the police; medical evidence was given by Dr. Paul, a legal physician. On the same evening, the newspapers brought the news to the Papal Nuncio, who telephoned directly to Rome. Well-informed persons say that the cause of the worker-priests was finally lost on that day.

30th May: The two priests, bearing the marks of their injuries, were received by Cardinal Feltin.

12th June: Monsignor Feltin issued a communiqué in which he expressed regret that the worker-priests had participated in this demonstration, condemned the actions of the police as an assault on human dignity, and rejected as pure libel a report in *Paris-Presse* which alleged that the Church had issued an ultimatum to the worker-priests, and that the priests had replied by saying that they preferred Communism to the Church.

14th June: M. Baylot, the prefect of Police, not knowing that Monsignor Feltin had personally interviewed the priests who had been assaulted, and seen their injuries, formally denied the 'false allegations', and regretted that the archbishop had not taken the trouble to verify the truth of the reports which had reached him.

On the next day he said: 'One could not expect him to disavow the activities of his subordinates'; and on the 4th July, when he was interrogated by the M.R.P. at the General Council of the Seine, he said that the two priests were lying.

July: The following passage appeared in an article by Jacques Fauvet published in *La Vie Intellectuelle*: 'Of course these two priests were "aligned"; that means that they participated by their acts, and not by their words alone, in the suffering and the hopes of mankind. Other Christians too are "aligned"—but in a way that gives a strange bias to our faith in the crucified Christ.' The anonymous editorial in the same issue added this comment: 'The Christian and the priest have good reason to join the labour movement, to protest against anti-Communism, to insist that in France Communism and the labour movement are bound together. But they must know that, when they do so, they are in danger of making themselves the playthings of a terrible reality, a cleverly constructed machine whose complex gearing they cannot, at their level, even begin to understand. It is true that the Christian worker, and the worker-priest, has through his immediate experience a knowledge of basic Communism which cannot be gained in any other way. But is he too engrossed in the immediate tasks of the day to be sufficiently well-informed about the party which makes use of its supporters, which takes possession of states, and which seeks to take possession of the world? By pointing out these dangers, we are not trying to save the capitalists, but rather to save the workers, the labourers and the humble folk, who are being exposed to a danger of enslavement of which present-day capitalism (though still to be fought) is only a mild foretaste'.

12th September: *L'Osservatore Romano* stated that 'The working-class movement is the one constant factor in the evolution of modern society, which involves the necessary decline of the capitalist phase and its replacement by a more just and more humane system of relationships'.

1953; 1st February: The worker-priests asked for a delegation to maintain permanent contact with the episcopacy on their behalf; to exchange information, to discuss, and to make appropriate regulations about current issues.

Cardinal Liénart referred the matter to Cardinal Feltin, who, though in agreement as to the principle, thought it would be a difficult matter to put it into practice.

29th March: Nineteen seminarians of the Mission de Paris, in spite of the interdiction of the Holy See, asked permission from their bishops to go to work; when they were refused this permission they in turn refused ordination.

3rd May: *Humanité* accused the C.F.T.C. of being in league with the government, big-business, and vested privilege. This declaration was signed by sixty-six people, of whom eighteen were worker-priests. It was assumed that they were falling under Communist influence—grouping together, compromising themselves, diverging from the Church.

8th May: News came from Marseilles that the archbishop had made a 'quasi-official' decision to recall his worker-priests. A priest wrote in reply: 'If we suppress the worker-priests we shall cut the Church off from the working-class. It is much more serious to suppress them than it would have been never to have had them in the first place. . . . What will become of the Church in Marseilles? The decision is particularly inopportune in view of the increased pressure which is being brought to bear at present against working-class militants. How will history judge this episcopal act? If Rome wishes it, then let Rome assume the responsibility.'

20th May: The Press gave great publicity to a report on the social situation in France, originally intended to be kept private which had been drawn up under the direction of Monsignor Richaud, at the request of the French hierarchy. The report stated that 'the profit motive is still the principle motive of activity among the *bougeoisie* and the employers.

'Profit margins are growing. . . . The purchasing power of the wage-earning classes has diminished, though the national income has increased. Among the wage-earners there is an atmosphere of class-conflict; they are aware that there is an opposition of interests between employer and employee arising from the very structure of capitalism, and that they have always had to resort to force to improve their conditions. The working-class malaise has a spiritual aspect; the wage-earners have a clear consciousness of their humanity, and of the human possibilities which are being denied to them.'

Cardinal Roques of Rennes wrote in *Aurore* : 'We are simply recording the facts; it is unlikely that we shall draw the conclusions we consider necessary without long and careful consideration.' *L'Osservatore Romano* (which had apparently forgotten its article of the 12th September quoted above), published a lengthy protest from anonymous Catholic industrialists against the findings of the French hierarchy.

23rd May : Six bishops received a delegation of worker-priests and asked whether the programme fixed by Cardinal Suhard had been modified. The worker-priests insisted that their work was being completely misunderstood. . . . Monsignor Guéry drew up an unfavourable report of this meeting.

27th May : The Archbishop of Marseilles forbade his priests to work. Two of them refused outright; the rest unanimously demanded an interview with the archbishop.

1st June : The new Papal Nuncio, Monsignor Marella, arrived in Paris.

27th July : Cardinal Pizzardo, Prefect of the Congregation of Seminaries, forbade any seminarian to undertake periods of factory work, because of the danger of moral and intellectual contamination. He said that this was an absolute prohibition, and no exceptions would be tolerated.

29th August : The Congregation of Religious sent a confidential circular to all superiors of Religious Orders :

'All those who have engaged in factory work or in any kind of labour with the permission of their superiors should be gradually recalled'.

6th September: The authorities announced to the 244 seminarians of the Mission de Paris that Rome had decided to close the seminary. The final-year students would however be allowed to return in October. The seminarians were asked to return to their families, or to join a group from the *Mission*.

23rd September: The Apostolic Nuncio called a meeting of twenty-six bishops and religious superiors at the archbishop's palace in Paris to convey to them the instructions of the Holy See.

4th October: Cardinal Feltin received two worker-priests, and told them: 'The Holy See is adamant that your Mission must be suppressed. We shall go to Rome. Rome also wishes for secrecy; but this will not be possible'.

Cardinal Liénart said that the suppression did not in any way resolve the problem, but only made the situation worse, causing grief to friends, and joy to enemies.

4th October: Four hundred militants of Workers' Catholic Action held a national meeting, and declared that this act of suppression of the worker-priests would be interpreted by the workers as a reactionary step showing a clear political alignment. The whole missionary work of the Church in France and the general action of Christians in the world was at stake.

10th October: On the occasion of the unveiling of a monument in memory of Cardinal Suhard in his own native village, Cardinal Feltin declared: 'In these critical days I have no other aim than to pursue the apostolic work of Cardinal Suhard—for he was a man of clear understanding.' Monsignor Chapoulie said on the same occasion: 'For Cardinal Suhard there was no other way to get in contact with the working-class masses than to climb over the wall, for the wall could not be removed. Priests must join the men in their lives, in their labours, and in their sufferings, just as the Son of God, through His incarnation, made Himself like us, His brothers.'

14th October: General Assembly of the cardinals and archbishops of France. The order of the day: the cardinals' journey to Rome concerning the matter of the worker-priests.

At this moment, *Réforme* insisted that there were too many positive elements in the work of the Mission for its suppression to be tolerated. Cardinal Feltin appealed in vain to Monsignor Marella to leave to the French hierarchy the responsibility of taking necessary measures.

After what we have been saying, this stand may seem to be surprising. Clearly the worker-priests made mistakes, and the hierarchy was by no means blind to these mistakes; it found the workers difficult to talk to, over-confident. Why should they be anxious to continue an experiment which had proved to be so dangerous and so complicated? Was the hierarchy itself, as some 'integralists' did not hesitate to affirm, sold out to the Communists?

To answer these questions we must again ask what it was that Cardinal Suhard had expected of the movement, and to what extent the worker-priests had fulfilled these expectations.

(1) *To arouse the Christian world and to give it a new sense of direction.*

Thanks to the worker-priests, we have learnt to know the workers' world from the inside; priests have crossed the barrier, and have shaken us by what they have said—by their reproaches, by their dogged determination, by their disgust. Through them, we have discovered a new world at our elbows, a world with its own culture and its own spirit, with the mood of a country in a state of war. From this world the Church is absent; and yet it has its own peculiar virtues of solidarity and simplicity which are close to the heart of the gospels. This is knowledge of capital importance for the orientation of the future apostolate; and it is the harrassed worker-priests who, by their much debated initiatives, have rendered the unique service of bringing this knowledge to the Church.

Thanks to them, we have also discovered how Marxism accords with the working-class mentality. Communism is realistic, and aims at real progress. The workers are in distress; Marxism demands action—and, of course, it is right.

For the past century and a half, the world has been going through a series of crises; first the emotional crisis of romanticism, then the intellectual crisis of scientism. The Church responded to the first crisis by the devotion of the Sacred Heart, and to the second by its vigorous intellectual initiatives. Each of these responses was adapted to the need of the time. Today, humanity is going through another crisis; this is the age of the unleashing of the instincts, which was predicted in the last century by Schopenhauer, and afterwards by Nietzche. Yet we remain immobilized in our out-of-date-intellectual structures, so that already a large part of humanity fails to understand us. We do not respond to its questions; we still talk 'truth', while it is asking us for *values*; we are still preoccupied with defending intellectual positions (necessarily so in intellectual circles) when the tide that is rising against us is no longer of the intellect or of the reason, but of the instincts. We are not being asked, 'Is all that true?', but, 'Is all that relevant? What is the *use* of Christianity?' The question appears to be an embarrassing one to some of our intellectuals.

Communism, on the other hand, starts with the instincts, with the ground of human reality. All our secret hunger and thirst for justice, our need for an ideal, our impulses of generosity, find a response in Communism—an incomplete one, certainly, but nevertheless a real response, and a concrete one. If we can do better, it's time we tried. Communism is a philosophy which starts from the fundamental needs of a whole body of people, and then leads them forward step by step through immediate and concrete objectives. It is a doctrine that works. This is the challenge which faces the Christian apostolate; we too must learn to be concerned with these same fundamental needs, and we too must propose concrete action. 'You cannot respond to a *mystique* by reasoning, but only by another *mystique*', wrote Abbé Godin. Are we prepared to meet this challenge?

This makes it easier to understand how intellectuals can accept Communism, in spite of its enormous intellectual lacunae. These are men of the 'instinctive' generation, men who have found in Communism a response to their vital needs; for this reason they are not greatly troubled by purely rational deficiencies.

The condemnation of the worker-priests should be the occasion for a profound examination of conscience. We can easily see that some of them made mistakes. Their Christian action had entirely admirable aims—but perhaps it was not the appropriate action for a priest, whose life should be directed entirely to supernatural activities. How many lives would stand condemned by such a judgement —lives devoted to teaching profane knowledge, to managing adolescents, to looking after accounts and business matters, to organizing entertainments, etc. etc.!

The worker-priests were accused of becoming too much absorbed in their activities, and of neglecting their lives of prayer; it was to preserve these lives of prayer that they were withdrawn from their dangerous engrossing apostolate. But Cardinal Lercaro, in his address to the Liturgical Congress at Assisi (8th-22nd September 1956) was speaking of the ordinary parochial clergy when he said, 'Many experienced spiritual directors of clergy complain about the ease with which meditation and other pious practices are abandoned; there is abundant evidence that today the Breviary is often totally or partially neglected, or else recited in a mechanical and ritualistic manner. . . .' Could it be that a large number of priests abandon their lives of prayer for motives much less substantial than those of the worker-priests?

In addition, the worker-priests were accused of falling under the influence of ideas contrary to those of the Church. We should however beware at this point of falling into the familiar error of the French, and believing that we have clarified a problem when we have made a few nice distinctions. (The point is well brought out by Fathers Lebret and Suavet in their book, *Rajeunir l'examen de Conscience*.) It is always simple to solve problems in theory. The Church condemns Communism: and the Church also condemns capitalism. Here then is the wretched worker: if he dedicates himself wholeheartedly to his cause, he will be excommunicated. Facing him, stands the crude exploiter, whose doctrine is equally condemned, enjoying a comfortable life at the expense of others; he, however, will not be excommunicated. Why? Because Communism is bad 'intrinsically', whereas capitalism is bad only 'per accidens'. . . .

To begin with, the worker-priests were well aware that their attitudes were equivocal, but they told themselves that these attitudes were the only possible ones, and then gradually came to believe whole-heartedly in them. . . . What of the rest of us? Canon Law, understandably enough, forbids priests to carry arms; in France, however, it is taken for granted that the Canon Law is not observed; and gradually, this non-observance becomes a custom.

Do our lay Christians accommodate themselves too readily to non-Christian society? Father Suavet wrote: 'All social institutions which habitually endanger physical, spiritual or family life, which deprive entire groups of the means necessary to sustain this life, or which place certain men in a state of inferiority, are frankly evil. Any institution, on the other hand, which favours liberty and responsibility, and which enables these qualities to be developed, has at least a fair chance of being good'.[3] That of course amounts to a condemnation of most of our society—the army, the factory, the living-conditions of our people, etc. etc. Nevertheless we all participate in this, we defend this 'order', even by violence, if necessary. From morning till night the Church in the West is being asked by the authorities to do all those things which are demanded of her behind the iron curtain —to perform public ceremonies, to bless official enterprises, and to exhort the people, in the name of religion, to resign themselves to the servitude which is being imposed on them from above.

So far as the major issues are concerned, however, the Church is not allowed the right to arouse the consciences of the people; if she dares to do so, then the blackmailing starts, in one form or another. So we have to be resigned to continuous compromise; what else is there to do? That is precisely the problem which faced the worker-priests; and, like us, they ended by believing that they were doing right by accommodating themselves to their environment. Unless we are going to be pharisaical about it, their condemnation (which was to some extent justified) should cause us a great deal of heart-searching. Subtle distinctions are used to salve the conscience: it is observed, for instance, that the priest-

[3] *Construire L'Eglise d'Aujourd'hui*, p. 29.

trade-union-official is in quite a different position from the priest-Député; the first is actually *sent* by the Church to carry out an apostolate, whereas the second is only *released* by the Church so that he can engage in politics. Distinctions of this kind are always available when conscience invites us to make unwelcome sacrifices.

The cardinals were aware of all these difficulties; that is why they did not wish to use double standards, to condemn one group without appeal, and to leave undisturbed another group which was equally guilty. The worker-priests had made mistakes, but they had obtained positive results which should not be forgotten or abandoned. The problem they had faced was still to be faced; the problem of how to enter this land of the workers, this country at war, without participating in its struggle. Other countries have been involved in wars—often in bloody wars, in unjust wars; and Christians and priests have been obliged to march with the others, to join in a struggle for an unjust cause, with means condemned by Christ and conscience. The more one reflects on these matters, the more complex they seem—unless they are resolved by using a double standard. That is why our cardinals tried to save an experiment which, for all its failures, had produced valid results.

(2) *The worker-priests had a second commission; to evangelize the working-class*

Did they fail completely in this second commission, by becoming exclusively involved in politics? Clearly not : one Jesuit-worker, when he was sacked by his employer because of his trade union commitments, was given a present of a chalice by his colleagues, in token of their affection and gratitude. These workers at least were able to see the priest in the trade unionist.

The following extract from *Franc-Tireur* was read with

surprise in many circles. It was written by a man notorious for his anti-clericalism.

'In this national crisis of conscience over the worker-priests, the laity could easily remain silent; they could say to themselves, "This measure which destroys the worker-priest could turn to our advantage; were they not our strongest rivals in the field of social action? We should take advantage of the situation". They could say this; but they do not. It is easy, when faced with the suffering of others, to preach resignation; it is harder, but much nobler, to go to those who suffer and suffer with them. By taking the second course, the worker-priests set a fine example. I would not wish to cause them further difficulty by injudicious praise; but it would be cowardly not to render homage to them. It is, after all, heartening to find that Frenchmen of such opposing views can still rally in support of certain supreme values'. (23rd February 1954.)

Morvan Lebèsque wrote in a similar vein in *Canard Enchaîné* (13th January 1954): 'There is this much to be said for these men : they did not stoop to the humble; they became humble with them. . . . They chose to see what others choose not to see : not the picturesque misery of yesterday, but the misery of today, the ultimate degradation of brutalizing mechanical labour without responsibility. St. Francis of Assisi, if he had lived today, would not have become a beggar; he would have become a miner, or a metalworker. Whatever their opinions, and whatever their ideals, I for one can have nothing but admiration for these men who took off their soutanes, rolled up their sleeves, and went to see what it was all about'.

The sad thing was that these unfortunate men did not know what was in store for them. They thought that they could master the misery they were to find; but it was the misery which mastered them.

71

'Through talking so much about spiritual bread, the Church had forgotten the material bread which supports it; and the worker-priests were therefore confronted with overwhelming realities which they had not learnt about in their seminaries. They discovered that the poor did not want words, but food; and that having grown tired of waiting, they were now beginning to take it; they had on their side the right of centuries of misery and slavery, of sweat and of hunger. The real bread which was neglected now has its revenge; now the ecclesiastical princes take fright, because the priests were sent to teach the poor, and it was the poor who taught the priests'.

Observateur, on the 4th March 1954, asked this question: 'Why is it that the *whole* of the Left is so intensely concerned over this affair? Not just the religious Left, but the atheists and the agnostics too—all seem to be passionately involved'. (Mlle Blanchet.)

We should ponder these passages, in which sincerity is mingled with hatred of the Church. It is not hard to see why we are detested; it is not hard to see that the worker-priests had begun to disarm the secularist opposition—and this was no small achievement. In spite of their imperfections, they were making contact with a world that was outside the church, and in conflict with it. These men of the 'lay' world, often sincere and generous-hearted, were waiting for a proof of the Church's sincerity, and they thought that they had found it; they were beginning to see the Church with different eyes. That is why the French hierarchy tried to save the experiment; in spite of mistakes, the results of the new apostolate already exceeded all reasonable expectations.

It would be fitting to conclude this chapter with the words of members of another faith, and another race:

'We are Moslems; when we arrived in France, we found

no one among our fellow-workers who believed in God. After a few years, we learnt of the existence of some priests of Aissa (Jesus), who lived with the poor, worked with their hands, and condemned with their lives and their words the worship of metal, as Aissa commanded.

'For them, we were not an inferior race. They regarded us as their equals in comradeship, and they talked to us as men. In the face of all the exploited and rejected North Africans, it now seems that this fellowship is to be destroyed'.

CHAPTER III

Reactions of the Hierarchy

In October 1953, the curtain went up on the first act of the drama of the worker-priests. Three conflicting theses were established:

(1) *Rome* inclined towards total suppression of the movement.

(2) *The worker-priests* (reflecting the majority view) thought that the Church was showing a Rightist mentality, an unavowed commitment to capitalism. In spite of their verbal protests, they believed that the authorities were really moved by a fear of Communism and of the rise of the working-class.

'Through the majority of its members and institutions, the Church is defending a régime which we, together with the working-class, are fighting with all our strength to overthrow, because it is a régime of injustice. The Church feels itself rejected along with the régime it is bound to; it is afraid of the rise of the proletariat, with all the changes this will bring to the lives and consciences of men; in particular, it is afraid of Communism, which inspires the rise of the proletariat, giving it its revolutionary vitality, and its future perspectives'.

(3) *The hierarchy of France* pleaded for the efforts of the worker-priests to be given sympathetic and brotherly consideration: 'The hierarchy has encouraged this experiment

74

in a completely new form of apostolate; but the priests engaged in it face grave dangers. They need our prayers and our affection, rather than our criticism' (Cardinal Feltin). The bishops took account of these dangers in an article published in the *Semaine Religieuse de Paris* (3rd October 1953); they were listed under four headings:

(a) The mission of the priest is a spiritual one; he must not therefore use 'human material, or political means'. Christ did not overthrow Caesar.

(b) It is an error to oppose the 'Church Spiritual' to the 'Church Hierarchical'.

(c) The law of charity is universal, and must extend to all races and to all classes. The class struggle may be a fact, but it is not inevitable.

(d) The preference given to personal judgement over the spirit of obedience encourages that form of neo-protestantism which the Pope most fears—especially as, during the enemy occupation, events worked out in a way that seemed to justify such an attitude.

The worker-priests had their replies to these criticisms. The cardinal was working in the realm of principle, the worker-priests in the realm of facts. Father Loew made a loyal and interesting effort to put the principles into practice, but even he did not avoid the condemnation of 1959.

'The tragedy of our generation', wrote Cardinal Feltin in the same article, 'is the gulf which separated the Church from the people. In spite of the apostolic endeavours of the Y.C.W. and other bodies, the situation has got worse rather than better; that is why France must now be regarded as a Mission Territory'. Cardinal Pizzardo, however, in his condemnation of the 24th June 1959, refused to believe in this de-Christianization of the working-class: 'It is hard to believe', he wrote, 'that those masses are de-Christianized of whom the majority have received the sacred and indelible

75

character of baptism'. Because the situation was not, after all, so very grave, the Holy Office considered that 'it was not necessary or possible to abandon the traditional concept of the priesthood, in order to evangelize the world of the workers'.

Nothing could show more clearly than this the lack of understanding between the worker-priests and the Holy Office. The disagreement was not over the way of answering the problem—such as whether priests should join trade unions—but over the way of *understanding* the problem. The Holy Office did not, in fact, believe that there was a fundamental cleavage between the Church and the workers; this was the fatal error.

For most of this century, and especially during the last thirty years, Christian sociologists have been drawing up report after report about the de-Christianization of the masses; but all that they could say was neutralized, in the eyes of the Holy Office, by the fact that many of the workers were still 'baptized'. Thus one party made its judgement on the grounds of observation, and the other focussed only on the 'sacramental reality'.

We can now follow the evolution of the drama between these three groups so remote from each other—the worker-priests, the French hierarchy, and the Holy Office. It was a tragic and a patient dialogue, patient on all sides; but it was doomed to failure from the outset, because of the differences of perspective which we have pointed out. If certain worker-priests did attempt the impossible, and try to link the demands of the Roman Church with the realities of the working-class, the Holy Office for its part did not visibly change its position. The condemnation, and the reasons invoked for it, in 1959, were exactly the same as they had been in 1953. The hierarchy did all it could to save the experiment by reforming it, by modifying it as much as possible so that it would meet the requirements of the Holy Office.

All this effort was in vain; and the basic reason for this was that the objectives of the two sides were quite different. The French hierarchy wanted to save the formula of the worker-priests, while the Holy Office was concerned only to rescue the formula of the 'traditional priesthood'. In view of this radical difference of approach, no mediator could have found a solution. The hierarchy strove for reform; the Holy Office strove for suppression; and this remained their attitude until the end of the play.

1953; 23rd September: The Apostolic Nuncio held a meeting of twenty-six bishops and religious superiors at the Archbishop's Palace in Paris to convey to them the instructions of the Holy See concerning the worker-priests.

5th November: Cardinals Liénart, Gerlier, and Feltin were received at the Vatican to confer with the Pope over the decision, which they wished to see modified. The audience with Pius XII lasted an hour and a half; the general impression, as Cardinal Gerlier put it, was of 'paternal benevolence, and filial confidence'. 'The Pope', he said, 'is disturbed by the de-Christianization of the working-class; he is however impressed by the view of certain theologians who consider manual work incompatible with the sacred state of priesthood.' He told the cardinals that he had stopped the experiment because it presented him with 'a grave problem of conscience'.

15th November: After receiving a reply from Rome, the cardinals published the following decision, which expressed the wishes of the Vatican:

'The worker-priests will be specially chosen by their bishop, and will be given a firm doctrinal formation.

'They will devote a limited part of their time to work (3 hours a day).

'They will leave temporal responsibilities to the laity.

'They will take part in the life of the parish.'

Apart from the two first decisions, which were inspired by necessary prudence, there are two points to note in this text :

(1) *The priests must not take part in trade union activities.* So the question is posed again; how can one belong to a country at war, without taking part in the war? Father Loew will find an answer to this.

(2) *The priests must take part in parish life.* This presupposed, of course, the right kind of parish, of which there were a certain number. Still, this regulation meant that the Mission de Paris must undertake a radical revision of its attitudes, for, ever since the time of Abbé Godin, it had been conceived as an extra-parochial organization. The worker-priests would have to leave their accommodation in order to live in the more 'open' parishes; not impossible, of course, but there would be serious difficulties.

(3) *The priests must not work more than three hours a day.* This meant that he could not be a 'worker' at all. The only option which was left open was for him to become an artisan; and that it what Monsignor Ancel and Father Loew did. But this was a serious change in the apostolate; from now on it would no longer be possible for the priests to be really present where the workers were, where they lived and thought. . . .

It was above all this last condition which seemed unacceptable. Father Chaillet wrote in *Témoignage Chrétien* : 'We must reconcile an authentic life as a worker with an equally authentic fidelity to the missionary spirit of the Church, and to the essential duties of the priesthood'. But how was an 'authentic life as a worker' to fit in with this pattern?

Father Villain, in *Etudes* (December 1953), expressed the

view that 'if the worker-priests agreed to renounce their temporal commitments, which were the source of all the trouble, an agreement could be reached on hours of work'. This is in fact what happened. Three hours a day was the limit first fixed by Pius XII when he spoke with Monsignor de Provenchère: but a few months later, he showed more understanding when he conceded to Cardinal Feltin, 'Do whatever is best; we place our confidence in you.' On the strength of this, Cardinal Feltin authorized six priests of the Mission to work full-time.

1st December: Cardinal Feltin declared that: 'The question of the worker-priests is one that concerns the entire world; this is clear from the letters we have received in this archdiocese. The positive results of the apostolate are incontestable; wherever there are worker-priests, their priest-hood has been efficacious. I have countless witnesses to prove how many individuals and families have returned to Christ through their ministry. But these men who live in a world dominated by the theses of Communism have necessarily breathed the atmosphere of their environment, with both good and bad results. It is understandable that Rome, which has been informed of the errors, should be disturbed. The institution of the worker-priests has now passed through its period of trial and experiment, and is reaching a critical point of decision. . . .'

9th December: Cardinal Grente, who was received by the Pope when he was passing through Rome, found him 'very satisfied' about his meeting with the French cardinals. On the same occasion Monsignor Grente expressed to the Pope his respectful protest against the excessive attention given to these 100 worker-priests, which caused people to forget the good work of the 30,000 who remained in the traditional ministry.

4th January: The debate flared up again over an

unexpected article by Cardinal Liénart in the *Semaine Religieuse de Lille*: 'Priest and worker have different functions, and different states of life, and these two states cannot be combined in a single individual without damaging the idea of the priesthood. The priest consecrates his life to God and to the ministry of souls; the worker carries out a temporal task'.

A comment in the *Observateur* read: 'What appeared to be merely a problem of internal discipline has now turned into a theological debate'. (28th January 1954.) A similar protest was voiced by *Actualité Religieuse*, which asked why there should not, in these days, be worker-priests, just as there were farmer-priests, financier-priests, scholar-priests, teacher-priests, and officer-priests? Jean Fabrègues replied in *France Catholique* that there was no reason why the worker-priests should be authorized to continue the errors which others had committed before them in different walks of life.

At about the same time Monsignor Ancel, presenting his respects to Cardinal Gerlier, in the name of the people of Lyons, said, 'We are confronted with a missionary problem the magnitude of which it is hard to conceive.'

1954; 19th January: Each worker-priest received a personal letter from his bishop, in which he was instructed, under threat of severe sanctions, to leave his trade union, to join a clerical group (not necessarily parochial), to give up the idea of forming a nationally organized team of worker-priests, and to limit his working day to three hours.

To this the bishops added, 'We dare not think what would be the consequences if you refused to submit. . . . You have spoken of "laicization". We must be frank about this; if you should ask to be reduced to the lay state, your request will not be granted. On the other hand, it is our duty to warn you that a priest who persists in disobedience is liable to canonical penalties. . . .'

The radical nature of the changes which were demanded, the short period of notice, and the threat of sanctions, immediately unleashed a furious onslaught in the Press. Cardinal Saliège protested: 'It is a sad business when inferior minds, who have received no higher education, attack our Holy Church in this manner'.

26th January: The bishops decided that the term 'worker-priest' should no longer be used, but should be replaced by 'mission to the workers'.

1st February: Father Yves Congar joined the ranks of the 'inferior minds, who have received no higher education'. In collaboration with Father Chenu, he wrote in *La Vie Intellectuelle* (February 1954): 'The condition of the working-class in our country is such that it is impossible to separate it from the struggle for its own liberation. Can we henceforth be *with* these people, even as a Church, without joining them in a battle which is fully in accord with the gospel, and with the redemption, transcendant but also real and concrete, of Jesus Christ? We must ask ourselves what is the Christian meaning of history; and the question must be brought down from the purely personal and spiritual level to the level of the collective history of mankind. The encounter with Marxism cannot be avoided; not with Marxism as a theory only, but with Marxism as the living ferment of the working-class struggle, continuously present and active in human lives.

'It is a simple matter to respond to the challenge of Marxism with a dogmatic "No"—a necessary step which the Church has not been slow to take. This still leaves untouched, however, the problems raised by the Industrial Revolution; they remain real questions, and there are valid elements in the real responses which have been made to them. We cannot derive everything from on high, by the simple application of dogmatic truths, deposited with us in an immutable form'.

At about the same time, the health of Pope Pius XII began to decline.

3rd February : Seventy-three worker-priests replied to the orders they had received from their bishops. In a brief communiqué addressed to the workers, and not to their religious superiors, they protested against the measures which had been taken, and declared that any compromise would be illusory and unacceptable. They announced that this collective reply would be supplemented by a letter to each bishop from the team of workers in his diocese.

7th February : Two hundred and fifty militant Christians from the Paris region presented an appeal to the hierarchy. 'In reality', they declared, 'what is being refused to these priests is not just temporal commitment, but commitment to the working-class'. (They also mentioned the priests who were teachers, officers, financiers, etc., whose commitment was accepted and blessed by the Church, while it forbade commitment to the working-class.)

8th February : Radio Vatican addressed the worker-priests : 'In general, your fellow-workers did not misunder-stand you; but outsiders misunderstood you. Your work has been misjudged by others; it will be continued in another form, but in the same spirit. Your greatness will be to say to yourselves that by your sacrifice, united to that of Christ, you will have worked better than ever before for the recon-ciliation of the workers to the Church'.

This formula will often be repeated—the same work is to be continued *'in another form'*; more and more this comes to mean quite simply : 'The traditional ministry'.

9th February : The day after this broadcast from Radio Vatican, the three Dominican provincials were deprived of their office, and four of the leading members of the Order were removed from Paris. On the following day, Cardinal Ottaviani, the pro-Secretary of the Holy Office, declared: 'France has been and continues to be the vanguard of the Roman faith; she has been, and continues to be, a Catholic country *par excellence*'.

Why were these steps taken? Father Avril was to write two months afterwards in *Amitiés Dominicaines*: 'Obviously more is involved than this one question of the worker-priests. For some time our general attitude to the present-day apostolate has been the object of criticism, attacks, and denunciations'. During this troubled period Father Chenu, Father Feret, and Father Congar respectively set out to reach a deeper understanding of 'priesthood', 'obedience', and 'the Church'; they all came under suspicion as 'dangerous thinkers'.

This measure provoked fresh reactions in the Press. Mauriac wrote in *Le Figaro*: 'To interfere with the work of the sons of Father Lecordaire in France, to inflict on them mortal injury, is morally equivalent to blowing up one of our great cathedrals'. He demanded a new concordat between the Holy See and France, which would protect the Church in France from the activities of the Roman congregations: 'I consider that it is in the real interests of the Church that, in a debate of this importance, she should have an opponent who has rights other than the right of silence'.

Monsignor Théas replied: 'Such self-determination would provoke nothing but scorn in other countries; French Catholicism is already anaemic—let us not stifle it altogether with the weight of our pride'. A Catholic *gaulliste* senator, Michelet, and the anti-clerical Déixonne, socialist *député* of *Le Tarn*, made the matter into a political incident, and asked the Minister of Foreign Affairs to intervene.

19th February: *L'Osservatore Romano* wondered whether those who spoke to Holy Church in this manner were showing a serious lack of faith, or 'a fundamental lack of psychological balance'.

20th February: All the worker-priests met at Villejuif for two days to decide what their attitude should be. On the day before, there was a meeting of 200 militants of Workers' Catholic Action, all members of a workers' community of Christian progressives at Montreuil. Jacques Madaule and Jean-Marie Domenach addressed the meeting, and a message was drawn up for the worker-priests, saying, 'The fate of the worker-priests is an overwhelming burden for us, because their problems are ours. We do not wish in any way to interfere in a decision which concerns only their own consciences; but we assure them that their fidelity to the working-class will never be for us a matter of scandal. It will not alienate us from the Church, but will rather spur us on to greater apostolic endeavours'.

22nd February: The Roman correspondent of *Le Figaro* observed: 'In Rome it is no longer a question of worker-priests; it is a question of obedience or disobedience'. This report seems to be confirmed by a speech of Cardinal Ottoviani, given on the 11th February at the Church of Regina Pacis in Rome, in which he condemned these 'reformers of the apostolate' who, under the pretext of going to the people, 'concerned themselves more with material bread than with the bread of heaven, and spoke little of Christ and His cross'.

He congratulated, on the other hand, the traditional priesthood, which was carrying out a prudent reform of the parish organization: 'Is there anything better, even in our time', he asked, 'than the parish?'

23rd February: Mauriac spoke out once more in the editorial column of *Le Figaro*: 'Can such a blow be struck, which will have lasting consequences in the lives of men, in the souls of priests, in the spiritual history of France and of the entire world, while the Holy Father is not with us— while Peter is not at the tiller, but present only as Christ was present, prostrate and asleep amidst the tempest?' (He alludes to the Pope's illness.)

25th February: Cardinal Feltin insisted in a pastoral letter that the worker-priests were not just playing a negative *rôle*: 'They did not expect immediate results; but their prayers and their sacrifices have borne fruit. In the first place, there are the numerous conversions, attested by an avalanche of letters from every sphere of society; but above all, by sharing the lot of their brother-workers, they have borne a testimony which has shone out far beyond the confines of their workshops, beyond the barriers which separate class from class, beyond the frontiers of France; their witness which has begun to dispel the prejudice that the Church of Christ is no longer the Church of the poor, but the servant of the rich'.

Why then were they suppressed? The cardinal gave this answer: 'In the first place, because deviations appeared, and it was known that, in view of the situation prevailing during the war and in the period immediately following, these men could not have received the complete doctrinal formation they needed'. The second reason, the cardinal went on to explain, was that the worker-priests were thrown into an environment which required of them not only generosity of heart, but also exceptional knowledge, in the social and economic as well as in the religious sphere. The third and most important reason was this: 'The meaning of the worker-priests' mission in the world required clarification. Unconsciously, their aims had been modified. Because of the confidence their colleagues placed in them they began to see themselves as arbitrators, counsellors, and then as militants and responsible trade unionists. They thought that, if they refused these risks and these responsibilities, they would be failing in solidarity with the working-class. Gradually, some of them allowed temporal activities to overshadow their spiritual concerns; and because of this, first the bishops, and then the Holy Father, felt it their duty to intervene. They understood the profound motives which inspired in these men a desire to identify themselves with the working-class; but it was their duty also to define the limits of this identification, in order that all should not fall into error and confusion, and in order that the laity as well as the clergy should have their proper definition. . . . When the Church sent priests into the world of the workers, she was asking them to carry out a priestly mission, in which they could not be replaced by laymen; it was a mission, therefore, which could not become identified with lay activities.'

The cardinal also clarified the point raised in the previous months by Cardinal Liénart. He was of the opinion that 'manual work is not incompatible with the priesthood'.

Finally, he made an indignant protest against the slanderous accusation that the decisions of the Church had been taken for political reasons; the Pope and the bishops, he said, were speaking as pastors, out of loving concern for the worker-priests, and to safeguard the primacy of the spiritual in their lives.

On the same day, *L'Osservatore Romano* published an article protesting against the theory that 'holiness favours revolution', and formally denied that the Church was bound to the *bourgeoisie*.

On the same day also, the health of the Pope began to give cause for serious concern.

25th February: The Roman correspondent of *France-Soir* sent a cable concerning the worker-priests: 'Renewal of experiment possible; no sanctions to be imposed'. Soon afterwards, Pius XII spoke in a similar vein to Cardinal Feltin: 'I place my confidence in you; do whatever is best'.

March: The Press started a guessing-game about how many of the worker-priests would refuse submission. These were their estimates:

France-Soir: Ten.

Observateur: A large majority.

Paris-Presse: Thirty-two.

Aurore: A small minority.

La Croix: 'We must be more discreet than ever—out of respect of consciences, out of understanding, out of sympathy.'

First days of March: Cardinals Liénart and Feltin and other prelates of the Church met at Rambouillet with about thirty worker-priests who had decided to obey instructions and give up work. These priests were anxious to keep the best relations with their recalcitrant colleagues. The bishops agreed to organize a workers' mission as quickly as possible in order to make use of the priests who had obeyed, and to call together, for some precise reason, those who still refused.

A plenary assembly of the French hierarchy was held in Paris on the 28th April, which led to the issuing of a *Pastoral Instruction on Social Matters*. It began by affirming that 'Christians must be present in the modern world in order to understand it, to love it, and to serve it'. It applauded the technical progress which had been made, but drew attention to the fact that many men were unable to profit from these advances, because of the abuses of liberal capitalism.

In a second section, the Instruction evoked the Christian attitude to civilization. 'The Church is not bound to any political régime, nor any economic system, nor to any particular form of civilization. . . . No political or economic régime can of itself bring to men all that they need to live in accordance with all the requirements of a rational nature'.

After a long attack on Marxism, a third section of the Instruction deals with the *rôle* of the priest. It underlines the supernatural and transcendant nature of the priest's mission; it denies him the right to set aside his religious mission in order first of all to remedy social evils. 'When a priest undertakes a more specialized task, he must take care to preserve the proper form of his priestly life, and, at the same time, keep the universal law of charity which is binding on him more than on any other'.

It is a priest's job to present the *Church's* social doctrine, and not any other. He must believe in resolving problems by evolution, and not by revolution. . . . He must refuse individual promotion, but work for the collective progress of the working-class.

15th August: The seminary of the Mission de France was authorized to re-open; it had a new canonical statute (with Cardinal Liénart as its first Superior), a new residence (the Abbey of Pontigny), and a new staff and training programme. This meant, in fact, a return to the classical seminary régime.

16th September: Twelve years previously, Father Michonneau had begun work in his first parish, the missionary community of Petit-Colombes; in 1947 he had begun to reform his second parish, that of SS. Peter and Paul in the same district of Colombes. Gradually, his influence had extended throughout the twenty-two parishes of the district of La Boucle. The priests in the area had become more open, more co-operative. It was to this area, therefore, that those priests went who wished to continue work with the cardinal's permission. There they set to work, circumspectly, to re-establish their mission in collaboration with the A.C.C. and the workers' parishes.

At the same time, Bishop Ancel founded in the Gerland district of Lyons a Pradosian community, whose income was to be derived entirely from the wages of its members. The bishop, who was also the Superior-General of Le Prado, himself took a job and became an ordinary working member of the community.

Meanwhile, a large number of worker-priests refused to submit. A few significant events should be noted:

7th March: A week after the notorious 'deadline' of 1st March, the final date for submission, Abbé Gouttebargue of Lyons was elected secretary of the large C.G.T. Union in the Department of the Loire. He wrote in *Le Monde*: 'I consented to my nomination, and therefore consented to accept the responsibilities which might result. The fact that the elections were by secret ballot makes me even less inclined to decline the position, and thereby betray the confidence which my colleagues have placed in me'.

19th March: Cardinal Gerlier wrote in a diocesan bulletin that those who refused submission were 'in a state of grave disobedience, with all the consequences which this implies for their priestly functions'. In addition, he said, they were manifestly deprived of the mission which the hierarchy had entrusted to them; they no longer represented the Church.

The cardinal explained that 'the mere fact of disobedience does not necessarily and immediately involve canonical sanctions; but if, by word or action, the disobedient priests should openly provoke authority, then clearly authority will have no alternative but to apply those sanctions which it earnestly desires to avoid'. After stating these general principles, the Cardinal addressed himself personally and solemnly to Abbé Gouttebargue, telling him that if he persisted in his attitude, the canonical sanctions would be imposed. . . .

Abbé Gouttebargue sent a letter of submission, and expressed his deep regret.

The progressivist review *Quinzaine* was condemned, shortly before the assembly of the national episcopate on the 13th March 1954.

Before the end of 1954, the worker-priests who were still recalcitrant published their own records in a volume called *Les Prêtres-Ouvriers*. A few days later, Cardinal Feltin protested against the publication of these documents, and 'for the last time' invited these priests to submit to the decisions which had been taken.

At their meeting on the 13th March 1954, the episcopate declared solemnly :

'It is false to assert that the Church has abandoned the working-class'.

'It is false to suggest that Cardinal Suhard had views which differed from those of the present hierarchy.'

'It is false to say that the recent measures were taken for political reasons or as the result of external pressures'.

'It is false to accuse the hierarchy of failing to guide the experiment, or of failing to warn the worker-priests in time of the dangers ahead'.

What reaction did this provoke among those concerned?

Thirty-one priests who were working on dam-construction gave this reply :

'Even in Rome, where the evolution of the movement was closely followed, it was not formerly considered that the conditions of a worker were incompatible with our priest-hood or with faith in the Church; yet now, brutally, we are asked to make a complete renunciation. Is it possible that we could not feel betrayed and cheated? The conditions which were imposed on us on the 1st March were harsher than anything we had been led to expect in our conversations with you. Our mission was precisely to remedy the narrowness of that discipline and training which you are now seeking to restore, because the religious authorities consider it more important to keep to this pattern than bring the Church into living contact with the most burning problem of our time. The goverment and the pro-government circles justify their policies by saying that there are more urgent problems than that of relieving the growing burden of misery. . . . Misery is pitied when it is without defence, but the authorities are disturbed to see the poor preferring the organizations which they have forged for themselves rather than those encouraged from above. The self-awareness and the force generated by these organizations seem to some Christians to be a greater menace to the Church than the loss of faith which once inspired their missionary zeal. . . .

'Before God who is your judge, you assure us, Your Eminence, that all this is not a matter of politics. We, however, think otherwise; the reality is infinitely more complex. But before God who is our judge, we assure you that you are destroying the very ground of our mission, in asking us to subscribe to your judgement. . . .

'You are asking us in effect to forget about the religious problems which we have had to face, and which are real only within the working-class. . . . It is in the light of our decisions in this present crisis that the working-class will judge us, and it is this decision which will give meaning to the years that have passed. Already you have revived a great scandal by re-calling us, a scandal which weighs heavily on the Church. What you call our 'temporal commitments' are in fact our commitments to the working-class, which we undertook with your agreement, and it is these commitments which you now ask us unilaterally to renounce, for reasons which belong to a world quite foreign

91

to the one we are committed to. This will not easily be forgotten.

'Certain persons, for reasons best known to themselves, are beginning to accuse us of refusing to discuss matters with the hierarchy. Your Eminence knows well that we have always considered you as our bishop, and that we have always been willing, especially during the last six months, to discuss with you our religious life, and the conditions on which it is based, and to share with you our mutual concern. You know that you have promised to do this, but have preferred to put off the occasion, and to confine yourself to public expressions of disquiet at opportune moments. We recognized in our loyalty to you that we had reached a point where further delimitation of our mission was necessary; but, far from consulting us over this matter, the authorities held aloof and presented us with a *fait accompli*. In full liberty, and in full loyalty, we confront your decision; but you present us with an impossible choice'.

One worker-priest wrote in *France-Soir*: 'Whether consciously or not, the Church is in fact influenced by political motives. At the time of the liberation, she gave permission for the worker-priest movement, because we were then in a progressivist phase. Now that we have entered a period of reaction, she disowns us and beats a retreat; with regard to the working-class, she is reverting to the Middle Ages'.

Finally, we quote the testimony of Father Perrin, a worker-priest first in Germany and afterwards in France: 'When we were forced to make this "impossible choice", some made a complete submission to the Church in the dark night of faith, hoping that once they had re-entered into a dialogue with the hierarchy, they would be able to obtain a revision of the official decisions; others, unable to break their bonds of loyalty with their fellow-workers, and ready to accept in faith the sanctions with which they were threatened, remained in their work, hoping in the darkness that one day, after a long wait, they and their brothers might once more find their place in the Church.

'I can only hope that this will make us realize to what extent Christians have failed to take account of the seriousness of the problem of the working-class. Year after year, the same pious phrases are churned out. I cannot think without sorrow of the letter of the General of the Jesuits in 1949, in which he lays down the apostolate of the working-class as "the principal object of the Jesuit Order". If this is the object, how pathetic are the results! The mountain in labour brings forth a mouse. Yet the *bourgeoisie* still disposes of the intellectual resources of the Society of Jesus, and is more and more enclosed in a ridiculous anti-Communist ghetto. . . .

'When we signed the communiqué (of the worker-priests), many people wrote to me to say how much they regretted its "Marxist tone". If there was such a tone, then this only proves that this tone is in no way inconsistent with our faith; did not St. Thomas start using the language of the Arab philosophers of his day, much to the scandal of his contemporaries? Whatever the appearances, this is not just "partisan" language; you can hear in it the echo of the class-struggle, but we are in fact living in a period of class struggle, just as surely as we are now at war in Indo-China—this is a truth which commands your assent as well as mine. If Christians are surprised to read this kind of language, this only proves that they are strangers to the working-class world.

'One thing is certain, and that is that we can never go back into the ghetto. My final words are that the issue is not one of obedience in faith. The Church takes certain measures which it judges to be expedient; that is its right. But it would be a great mistake to think that goodwill can resolve all problems, and that the great gulf which separates the Church from the working-class world can ever be filled without an earthquake which will shake the foundations, and cause the Church to suffer as Christ did in His agony.

'The spirit of submission will not solve all the problems which face us; and once these problems become real to us, a man's first loyalty to his conscience is to face them. No one can deny that, in the depths of his conscience, it is God who judges.

'I do not wish to repeat what I have written about so many times—the distress of millions of souls, whether Catholics or not, who through us had begun to catch a glimpse of Christ in the Church. Rome judged that this should be discontinued; let it be so. But the history of our movement is fraught with heavy consequences; too many things have been done which are not of God—by us, alas, but also by those who govern the Church. . . . Tomorrow, the drama will continue in the minds and consciences of thousands of Christians, especially priests, where it mingles with the other dramas which are already troubling the waters.'

If these words give evidence of terrible spiritual suffering, it is because the worker-priest had been rejected; in the words of Mounier, 'to despair of a man is to drive him to despair'.

Father Perrin did not question the priesthood itself; but, like so many others, he did question his own priesthood. When he was suddenly removed from this life in a motor accident in that tragic year, 1954, he was carrying in his pocket a letter asking if he could be reduced to the state of a layman. It had been in his pocket for a fortnight, unposted. The Lord Himself resolved the tragic conflict. But how many suffered this same conflict, and were forced to resolve it by themselves?

A book about the work of Father Perrin ends with this question :[1] 'How is it that a priest of the Church should thus have come to think of renouncing his priesthood, his unique vocation of bringing together his brothers and his God—the workers and the Church? It was his whole life that was at stake.'

We cannot help being disturbed as we read the evidence, and become aware of the agony of that year. Can one doubt the sincerity of authority, in stressing what was after all its central concern—the priesthood of the worker-priests? In asserting that the priesthood was a special vocation, in view of a supernatural function, the authorities were manifestly guided by theological principles, and we know that they were right. At the same time, we are disturbed by the firm conviction of the worker-priests that these same authorities were influenced by political considerations.

This is a serious accusation. To substantiate it, one would require irrefutable proof—not just a vague antipathy towards the ecclesiastical world in general, or towards the Vatican in particular.

One thing is certain first of all : and that is that the Roman authorities were certainly not carrying out a political manœuvre when they became concerned about the priesthood of the worker-priests. The priests themselves were the first to admit that there were reforms to be made, and precautions to be taken; that their way of life must be modified. Father Loew said that Rome had sensed something from afar, with a supernatural instinct—even though she was not aware of the details of the concrete situation, and of all that was involved in it. (*Journal d'une Mission Ouvrière*, pp. 243-245.) There is a secular experience of Rome which is reminiscent of the Holy Spirit, watching over the actions of the Church.

[1] Editions du Seuil.

Nor was it political motives which caused the French hierarchy to write in its Instruction of 1954: 'When a priest undertakes a more specialized task, he must take care to preserve the proper form of the priesthood, and to keep the universal law of charity which is more binding on him than on any other'.

These theological principles were too often forgotten in the heat of the discussions; the Church called them to mind, and she was right to do so. There can be no doubt that these same principles had a great influence on the decisions which were finally taken. It is absolutely false, therefore, to reduce the whole matter to the level of politics.

On the other hand, we must take account of political imperatives. For fifteen years, the Right has used every possible means to discredit the worker-priests—with the French people, with the French bishops, and with Rome itself. Any method was considered justified which could achieve this end, and every possible method was exploited; the Holy Office itself supplies evidence of this as early as 1945. The bishops and priests of France were inundated with propaganda. The public knew of it through the newspapers. Father Loew himself, while applauding the 'supernatural instinct' of the Church, observed also when he went to Rome that the big industrialists—intelligent, organized, and economically unassailable—were exercising an enormous influence in high quarters: '*They* travel to Rome; they defend their positions. . . . *We* talk of matters which touch the heart—we bring reports of the horrors of this or that factory; but we bring no systematic and scholarly survey, which would start with facts and draw well-founded conclusions.'

To what extent did these influences affect the decisions of the Holy Office? Could there possibly be any evidence which would enable us to answer such a question?

It is sometimes observed that the parable of the wheat and the tares (Matt. xiii) by which Christ describes the Kingdom of God, applies to all ecclesiastical work. Everyone knows, for instance, that some of our leading anticlericals are former pupils of our Catholic schools, and that they proclaim to all and sundry that they lost their faith in those very institutions which were designed to foster it. The positive results of Free Education and Catholic Schools however are considered sufficiently important to outweigh the inevitable failures. Why then should the Roman authorities suppress the mission of the worker-priests, in which good and bad were also mingled, and not suppress the free schools which produce equally mixed results?

What the Holy Office wished to assert by its abrupt decision, was that the priest is first of all a priest; that his work is first of all of the spirit, and that worldly causes, however just (and they are usually very imperfectly so) must never be allowed to overwhelm his priestly activities.

André Frossard wrote in *L'Aurore* (24th February 1954): 'It would not be easy for the Pope to concede that the re-Christianization of the workers could only be achieved by the de-Christianization of the priests. Yet to choose a certain party, or a certain trade union, is already to be slightly de-Christianized. The Lord never walked round the walls of Jerusalem, crying "Pilate is a murderer!" or "Down with Caiaphas!" François Mauriac has been telling us for months that politics is "essentially impure"; and common sense tells us that he is right. A political priest is a diminished priest'.

Teilhard de Chardin replies: 'In order to act effectively in any current of life, you must belong to the current; only a worker can be understood by workers; only a geologist or a soldier can talk to geologists and soldiers. Only a man can command an audience of men'.

97

In real life we seem to be cornered by these two attitudes. In the dilemmas which result, it is the delicate task of authority to make decisions. What it seeks above all is to preserve the sacred character of the priesthood, and to recall the priest to his supernatural ministry, and to an exclusively priestly frame of mind.

Is this a doctrinal and pastoral position—or is it a political manœuvre? The whole of the Left was asking this question. Why had the *worker*-priests been singled out for this rigorous treatment, rather than others?

'The worker-priests are condemned; but what of the priest-officers, the priest-journalists, the priest-politicians? For two years, by order of my superiors, I did the work of a layman in a school, teaching mathematics and physical science to senior forms, while at the same time I was in charge of two parishes. Often a priest's work is to take charge of ten pupils (sometimes less), members of the *"bourgeoisie"*, or the "future *bourgeoisie*", and instruct them in purely secular matters; and what are we to think of the priest who is a private tutor in a single family?' (Henri Dubois, parish priest of Lège et Burgalaye, Haute-Garonne).

During the crisis of the worker-priests, the bishops of France declared that 'the Church was not bound to any party'. But we must endeavour to understand both sides with equal clarity if we are not to stand condemned by the accusations of the Left, who reproach the authorities for acting according to political preferences, or at least according to political necessity.

'You served the Roman Emperors; you served the feudal Lords; you served the absolute monarchs; you served the triumphant *bourgeoisie*. You have always (though not without subtle manœuvres to show your independence and superiority) been on the side of the strongest, and you have made yourselves even stronger than they by your pretence

98

of defending the weak. What is your policy now?—to take
to yourselves the cause of Man, the cause of the weak of
yesterday, who are to be the powerful of tomorrow? The
device is too crude, the morsel is too large to swallow. For
the first time, the stomach of Holy Church, which has
digested all in the past, may not be able to stand the strain.
She knows it; and she trembles. She plays a double game—
a triple game—but still we see through it!'

This is the judgement of a Communist, Henri Lefèvre, on
the general conduct of the Church;[2] and it is a judgement
which can only be countered by acts—not by solemn
declarations, but by deeds which prove conclusively that
the Church is *not* bound to any political party, and that
it has no political inclination of its own.

Are the men of the Left and the men of the Right within
the Church prepared to lay aside the options which divide
them, and read together these words of P. F. Simon?

'There are certain priests who show a striking affinity
with men of the military profession. Not that they feel
attracted to the violence of militarism; I presume that in
their innermost souls their charity remains entire. But those
same authoritarian and doctrinaire aspects of their personalities, which are encouraged by their ecclesiastical garb,
flourish equally well beneath a soldier's uniform. The habit
of submitting a collective ethic to a clearly defined rule of
faith, of distrusting common sense and personal fantasies,
and identifying justice with the service of a cause superior
to the interests of the individual, all this means that the
individual who exercises authority in the Church has a
magnificent training for manipulating the machinery of
discipline in the army. Nothing is easier, once you have
become part of this great machine, than to acclimatize
yourself to the passions which govern it, and to convince

[2] *Critique de la Vie Quotidienne*; Introduction, p. 232.

yourself that the war you are fighting is certainly just, and willed by God.

'The military activity however, because of its spice of danger, and because of the physical strength and courage which it calls for, has something manly and exciting about it, which is exhilarating for those who have been secretly frustrated by the customs and the costumes of the ecclesiastic. . . . The Church is surprisingly tolerant towards the lay government, when it requires clerics, contrary to the rule of canon law, to use firearms; but there is no doubt that this new profession has a strong appeal for many of them. You only have to call a war a "crusade", and all difficulties are resolved'.

Simon admits that there are many whose priestly character makes the military atmosphere quite intolerable for them; but he sees on the other hand a by no means rare type of military chaplain who carries out his functions in a way that makes him a redoubtable combatant. His concern is to maintain the 'moral forces' of the men; or, more exactly, to mobilize the religious consciences of the men, to confirm their courage and consecrate their military duty. . . . Thus reassured about the ends of the battle, they are equally confident about the means. . . .

'It is of course a great convenience to have at hand a "director of souls", who is ready to authorize in the name of the Word of God and of human wisdom the rules of action which have in fact emerged from the pressure of circumstances, instinct, and self-interest. The warrior-priest is no doubt thinking primarily of his warrior role; one might wish that he paid a little more attention to his priestly one. In the final analysis, he has no scruples of personal responsibility —he has not even the simple reflexes of pity and honour which disturb the conscience of believers and non-believers, of the uneducated, the lay teacher, the Paris metalworker, and the Breton conscript. . . . I would not say that the soul of the Church has disappeared altogether from his mind, plastered over as it is with references, definitions and syllogisms; but it is hard indeed to discern its presence'.

This long quotation seems to me justified because of its relevance to the problem of the worker-priests. The workers are by instinct anti-militarist, and would readily applaud all that Simon says; they would be right to protest against the impure elements which infect the spirit of the priesthood when it is placed in a military environment.

Yet, if we replaced the words 'soldier' and 'warrior' with the word 'worker', we should have here a disturbingly authentic picture of some of our worker-priests. It is by the faults of others that we learn to understand our own.

The men of the Right have also something to learn from this text. They are anti-revolutionary, and often anti-working-class; they applauded the decisions of the Roman authorities against the temporal commitments of the worker-priests, and they congratulated the Church for recalling them to a sense of their supernatural vocations. In this they were right. Let them not forget, however, that in their own circles there are many instances of these same deviations, of this same abuse. The Right as well as the Left has its risk for the priesthood. The problem cannot be avoided by subtle intellectual distinctions; everywhere the priesthood must learn to break ties, for spiritual independence is a vital necessity.

CHAPTER IV

The Search for a New Formula

ON THE 23rd September 1953, Monsignor Marella, the Papal Nuncio, made known to the French episcopate the decision of the Holy See to suppress the worker-priests.

The French bishops did all they could to save the experiment, by reforming it, and by searching for a compromise between the requirements of the working-class mission and the decrees of the Holy Office. By agreement with Pope Pius XII, some worker-priests who had submitted were later allowed to resume work under obedience, providing certain conditions were fulfilled.

Father Loew's efforts to work under these conditions are of particular interest, since, long before the condemnation of 1953, most of his views corresponded closely with those of the Holy Office.[1] Father Loew was the first to see the movement as a whole. Hiss mission had originally been to take a job as a worker, and to carry out, in conjunction with *Economie et Humanisme*, a socio-religious survey. What he succeeded in doing, however, was to establish a great missionary enterprise, and to integrate it into the organization of a working-class parish. In addition, he established in this parish a centre for the training of future worker-priests—or rather, as he would prefer to put it, of future priest-workers.

[1] J. Loew. *Journal d'une Mission Ouvrière*, Edit. du Cerf, Rencontres, 1955.

The philosophy of Father Loew shows how false it is to generalize about the 'worker-priests' and to pass mass-judgements on them. Father Loew was quite different from most of them in his intellectual views, and in his attitude to the world, the apostolate, and the priesthood.

(1) *Father Loew's intellectual attitudes*

Father Loew was an intellectual. He started work as a lawyer in Nice; then he became a convert, and had a late vocation to the priesthood. Thus he followed up his studies of Law and Politics with a solid theological and philosophical formation in the Dominican Order; and his subsequent collaboration with *Economie et Humanisme* gave him in addition the skill of a professional sociologist.

In him, then, the wishes of Cardinal Suhard were fulfilled —that a worker-priest should have a 'sound and appropriate intellectual formation'.

His views were much more subtle than those of many worker-priests. He did not talk of the 'soul of the proletariat', or of the 'will of the proletariat', or of the 'hope of the proletariat', as if these were simple identifiable objects. He knew that these terms covered a very complex reality. In his theology, he was concerned with the crucial distinction between the Kingdom of God and the worldly society founded on justice; between terrestrial happiness, and eternal salvation; between evangelization, and the mere presence of priests and militants. To read him is an intellectual tonic. Before he begins to debate any issue, he clarifies the terms, and shows clearly what is at stake. He knows about the confusion which reigns in the minds of many Christians, and puts them on their guard against what he calls 'superimposed photographs'.

In opposition to the progressivists, he does not admit that 'working-class' necessarily means 'Marxist'. He does not consider that Marxism even satisfies the true aspirations of the workers themselves; it is only a hardened and restricted expression of a greater ideal.

Instead of saying 'every worker is a Marxist', he takes care to distinguish three aspects of the working-class man :

(a) The mechanized man: 'People of our time are mutilated by their conditions of life. The obsession with production and profit, which seem inescapable as soon as large-scale capital is involved, the factory and workshop environment where everything is man-made, and where there is no contact with the living realities of nature . . . all this is a serious handicap for anyone seeking spiritual food. *Homo faber* has ousted *homo sapiens*; and *homo faber* is himself being ousted by *homo animal*, who lives only for his body (witness the advertisements in the underground). If Marxism awakens a profound response, it is because it is a desperate effort to organize this mechanical world, and to get the best out of it. But Marxism has shut itself up in this prison, and lost the key. Only the Church possesses the key.'

(b) The Marxist man: 'If we identify Marxism with the working-class, and see in it the adequate expression of the conscience of the proletariat, then we are forcing the evidence; but the basic premisses of Marxism, and even more the Marxist reflexes, have certainly begun to take possession of the minds and the bodies of the workers of our time.

'Marxism appears to them as the natural (Marx would say necessary) expression of the ordinary observation of the man-in-the-street. The dialectic of the class-struggle turns into a universal law, governing the whole of human society and even the world of matter, and confirms in men's minds the belief already supported by countless little experiences, that without the working-class struggle there will be no real advance towards greater justice.

'At the same time, the perfectly legitimate aspiration to

a greater degree of material well-being is swallowed up in a system in which it is only the economic values which count. Above all, the vague ideas born of laicism and scientism ("it's all over when you're dead"; "evolution explains everything"; "animals are intelligent too", etc. etc.), judgements spontaneously accepted without analysis or investigation, find a certain cohesion in the philosophy of materialism, and acquire a new vitality.

'All this penetrates the minds even of those who are anti-Communists, and supporters of Christianity; and, to an immeasurably greater extent, it moulds the mentality of those who have embraced Communism whole-heartedly, who have been completely taken in by the "religion of this world", with its rites, its commandments, its grandeur, its heroes, its excommunications, and its Absolute of the world and tomorrow.'

(c) The man who knows only a caricature of religion: 'This man in whom the sense of God has been stifled by a mechanical environment and by a hostile philosophy, nevertheless thinks that he has a clear idea of religion and of faith. On investigation this idea turns out to be a grotesque caricature.

The man we are talking about is not just 'without God and without hope'; he *thinks* that he knows the God of the believers—the God of compulsory Sunday Mass-hypocrisy, the God of fish-on-Fridays, the prayer of the lips, the religion of mechanical rewards from heaven, the religion of money and of *bourgeois* oppression; what he sees is empty formalism without spiritual substance, mechanical practices whose religious meaning is obscured, but which effectively prevent him from suspecting the existence of a worship in spirit and in truth, of a religion of love. As for the Church and its priests—it would be better not to speak of them.

'He looks for the religious virtues (devotion, dedication to

105

an ideal greater than oneself) in the trade union movement; for it would never even enter into his head that he could find them in the Church.'

Father Loew concludes: 'Before we can build, we shall have to sweep away all this rubbish, or the foundation stones of the gospels will remain buried beneath the debris. That is why the Mission must be fearless about breaking with certain external forms, which, far from being signs leading to faith for the man in the street, only seem to him so many lies. The worker-priests moved public opinion profoundly, not because they had become involved in the temporal, but because they seemed, in the eyes of the people, to be *men of truth*.'

When we read this, we may call to mind the second objective of the Mission as defined by Cardinal Suhard in its early days: the reform of the traditional Christianity of the old parishes. The Mission had never directly undertaken this task. Father Michonneaux made it his special concern. Father Loew, finally, in the parish of La Cabucelle de Marseilles, conceived the possibility of combining the workers' mission with the work of parochial reform.

(2) *His choice of the parish*
After 1947 Father Loew was at once a worker-priest and a parish-priest. He worked out a rota with his curates, so that they could spend part of their time in the parish, and part of it among the workers.

As a result of this system, the workers had 'comrades' in the presbytery who understood their problems, and spoke their language. In the eyes of their fellow-workmen, they were still 'priests'; it was they who celebrated marriages, and officiated at the local funerals. Occasions for making contact with the supernatural were rare in the factory; but they were common in the parish, where the same workers and the same priests were to be found. By comparison, the worker-priests who lived outside the parish structure had a much more restricted field of contact.

How many worker-priests would be needed to serve the whole of the working-class in this way?

The presence of a worker-priest in a classical parish is equally valuable for the 'regular parishioners'; he makes it impossible for them to ignore any longer the problems which face the Church—they can no longer dream away in their pious 'tranquillity'. He is a representative in their midst of that 'barbarous people' who are waiting at the doors to be admitted. If they are to be given a proper welcome, the house must be made ready by priest and people; an inventory must be made of old traditions, to see which will help and which will hinder the reception of the neophytes. Here Father Loew advocates the same reforms as those which were proposed by Father Michonneau in *Paroisse, Communauté Missionaire* : the abolition of 'classes', a truly communal and comprehensible liturgy, preaching which is 'really addressed to someone' (Cardinal Saliège), etc. Even more emphatically than Father Michonneau, Father Loew insists that there must be a Directory of the Sacraments adapted to the society of 'practising non-believers'. He does not wish to refuse the sacraments to the 'baptized', but he requires of them sufficient religious knowledge to 'know what they are doing'—a requirement fully in accord, of course, with canon law. Father Loew prefers not to administer the sacraments to those who regard the sacred rites as a form of folk-lore, and he wishes to begin at the beginning with basic instruction. In this way, he thinks, our 'traditional parish', which is at present only a hollow imitation of a former Christianity, will gradually become a real Christian community again, brought to life in the midst of the twentieth century.

The word 'community' of course raises the crucial issue. A genuine community is not formed in a day. 'Community' means 'sharing'—it means a common life, a common task, a common will. How can this community be formed in a parish between 'old Christians' of various social classes, and militant neophyte workers?

The workers themselves imposed four conditions:

(a) The priests should encourage Christians to take a greater part in the working-class struggle, and to work with Communist militants.

Father Loew replied: We can *invite* Christians, but we cannot compel them or impose a duty on them. Collaboration with the Communists is impossible for an isolated Christian, because he is sure to be 'taken in' in the long run.

(b) The priests should never criticize working-class organizations, such as the C.T.G., in case they offend working-class sensitivities.

Father Loew replied: We are not partisans; we must be free to say what we think—to denounce evil wherever we find it.

(c) The priests should not start anything without first consulting the militant laity.

Father Loew replied: Of course the laity must be consulted, and real importance must be attached to their point of view; but they in their turn must realize their limitations. They may be well able to cope with the problems of the working-class struggle; but they may not be so good at finding the exact solution to a religious problem.

(d) All action decided on must be undertaken together by the workers and the *bourgeois* of the parish.

Father Loew replied: This touches the main problem, but it must be stated correctly, or it will be quite insoluble. The real question is, what will be the class structure of the world of tomorrow?—and this is a question of politics.

Everyone has something to hope for—perhaps the rule of the proletariat, perhaps an improvement in the present régime—or perhaps (could it be possible?), a third solution, a world in which every one will have his place.

'One prefers revolution, another reform. Again, no one's solution is going to be imposed in the name of Christianity. The only thing which Christianity imposes is the duty of everyone to work for a better world'.

Consequently : 'In the social or political sphere I adopt a particular remedy for a particular injustice because, in view of the whole situation, I judge it to be the most effective, and in conformity with the moral law and with the Christian faith. I take care not to christen this particular course of action "The *Christian* answer".'

Let those of use who speak so glibly of the 'parish community' meditate on the words of St. Paul : 'There is neither Gentile nor Jew, circumcision nor uncircumcision, Barbarian nor Scythian, bond nor free. But Christ is all in all.' (1 Cor. xii. 12-13; and esp. Col. iii. 11.)

We have not yet faced this problem squarely in our Christian communities; we think of our fellowship in Christ more as a balm to assuage injuries after they have occurred, than as the very basis of our living together, the foundation of our faith, and the touchstone of genuine Christianity. . . . The unity of the community is the sign and the effective cause of the presence of Christ within it, and it must be shown in a concrete change of behaviour. If there are Christians who are clearly doing wrong they must be told about it. The procedure is laid down in the Gospels.

(3) *The choice of the priesthood*

Father Loew, like Father Voillaume, the founder of the Little Brothers of Jesus, thought that it was better to 'sacrifice the unity of the working-class, even though this makes for rapid results, in order to be free to hold a Christian view of labour'. They were both convinced that it was possible to be a true worker, and to share the great aspirations of the working-class, without becoming a Marxist. 'We must learn to assert both our solidarity with the working-class, and our inability to model our actions on evolutionary materialism'. (R. Voillaume.)

This in an open rejection of progressivism. It concedes to the Marxism the need to emancipate the working-class— but denies that Marxism can do this.

How then is one to show solidarity with the working-class? Fathers Voillaume and Loew are in agreement about this too : by membership of trade unions, by joining in mutual aid and collections which do not have an obviously political purpose. Even membership of the C.G.T. would be legitimate—so long as it did not mean being taken in by Marxism.

Father Loew considers that the worker-priest who lives, works, and suffers with his comrades has no need to show his solidarity by entering into politics in the same way as a lay militant. 'The masses are already convinced that the Church represents the politics of reaction; now we suggest that it should become involved in the politics of democracy! If there were militant trade union priests, the masses would certainly draw the conclusion that the Church was still involved in politics.

'Of course the worker-priest must join the union which defends the workers. But he must not go any further— priests must not become politicians.'

Father Loew considers that the priest contributes in his own special way to the workers' struggle for justice. The Word of God is a sword which pierces the mind and heart; the priest's work is that of the prophet, who proclaims the Truth, welcome or unwelcome. This is neither an easy task nor an ineffective one; it is a lonely mission, which, when

carried out with holiness, can put whole armies to flight—
witness Gandhi. The working-class itself, if it is to remain
morally sound, needs men who do not belong to any party,
and who because of this can declare clearly what is just,
and what is unjust. Those who are busily engaged in the
building of a city have a secret fear of the prophet who, in
sovereign independence, denounces the wrong which lurks
in the shadows.

If a priest were to come down into the political arena,
would he not be betraying his mission?

The priest of the workers has yet another task which no
one else can do in his place; and that is to bring the supernatural to his brothers. One might ask, how is it possible to
feed those who are not hungry? It is of course hard for the
workers to show a desire for spiritual food which is unknown
to them. Nevertheless, some worker-priests did manage to
hold meetings of small groups of workers to read and comment on passages of scripture. One must sow today and reap
tomorrow.

(4)   *The priest and factory-work*

Father Loew was all that Rome wanted a worker-priest to
be. He questioned the attitude of the Holy See on one matter
only—that of the length of the priests' normal labouring day.
He pointed out that it is by working that you really belong
to the working-class—become a brother of the humble of
this world, not in words alone, but also in deed. The Jewish
Rabbis worked with their hands, and regarded this as
normal, at a time when Greeks despised manual labour as
the work of a slave. It was in this historical setting that St.
Paul, a Roman citizen, became himself a worker-bishop.

The priest today has to face a prejudice similar to that of
the Greeks. The *bourgeois* would be horrified to think that a
son of theirs should have to work with his hands; and even

the workers themselves are ready to make all kinds of sacrifices so that their sons can stay on at school as long as possible, to escape from the curse of working-class existence, and to have a different kind of life from that of their parents.

It is customary to congratulate St. Paul for restoring the dignity of manual work in the eyes of Roman society; could not the priest of our times have a similar role? By sharing the real poverty of the workers' condition, could he not give to the humble that proof of love which they must have if they are ever to believe in the sincerity of the Church?

The priest of course is worthy of his hire: 'If we have sown unto you spiritual things', said St. Paul, 'is it a great matter that we reap your carnal things?' And yet, knowing the mentality of the Corinthians, he hastened to add: 'But I have used none of these things. Neither have I written these things, that they should be so done unto me; for it is good for me to die rather than that any man should make my glory (the glory of the gospel) void.' (1 Cor. ix. 3-18.) 'Even unto this hour we both hunger and thirst, are naked, are buffeted, and have no fixed abode; and we labour, working with our hands.' (1 Cor. iv. 11-12.) 'I will not be burdensome to you; for I seek not the things that are yours, but you.' (2 Cor. xii. 14.)

The workers are convinced that the priest is a profit-maker, an idler, a good-for-nothing. It is impossible to remove this prejudice, which is an absolute barrier to any evangelization, without effective proof in acts. It is the priest more than anyone else who has the right to say to the professional idlers, who fit in a visit to the presbytery between two visits to the wine-merchants, 'If any man will not work, neither let him eat . . . for we did eat no man's bread for nothing; but in labour and in toil we worked night and day, lest we should be chargeable to anyone'. (2 Thess. iii. 8 and 10.)

112

It might be thought sufficient to practice a craft or a trade; but if the priest wishes to exercise a real influence on the workers' environment, he must live, think, and work where the worker lives, thinks, and works—and that is in the factory.

What factory would take on a priest to work a three-hour day? Surely it would be possible to arrive at some agreement with the Holy Office, on the principle of a full day's work, but in rotation?

This was in the mind of Father Loew on the eve of the second condemnation.

(5) *A centre to prepare workers for the priesthood*

This was the last point in Father Loew's programme. Experience had shown that it was difficult for a priest from a *bourgeois* environment to adapt to the workers' mentality; and it is regarded as the object of every mission to foster 'native vocations'. People in a mission territory are always deeply influenced by the promotion of one of their number to the dignity of the priesthood. The problem is similar with the workers' mission. There were, of course, odd examples of workers who had late vocations and became priests; but their seminary training had estranged them from their former environment. Many, on the other hand, who thought they had a vocation, were forced to give up because there was no scheme of training in any way suited to their mentality.

Father Loew quotes in his book (pp. 383ff.) from two of these 'worker-seminarians':

'From the first day I tried to do everything that my superiors asked. I must confess, however, that there were some things that I could never do with any sincerity, despite all my efforts. Here are a few examples which spring most readily to mind:

113

'I could never completely rid myself of habits of working-class speech. I could never speak to my former mates with the formal politeness of *bourgeois* etiquette. It was always painful for me, after the warm comradeship of Action Catholique Ouvrière, to live in the frigid individualism of the seminary cell, where everyone works away in his corner at his own perfection, not knowing whether his neighbour is an orphan, or an only son, or whether his family is happy or miserable.

, 'It was also distressing to see that not only was no account taken of great or small responsibilities which one might have carried before coming to the seminary, but that one was treated like a small child who has to be watched—all the time in case he does something naughty. The hardest trial of all, and the one that was for me quite impossible, was the effort to dress up in a *bourgeois* culture and education which was totally foreign to me. It seemed to me that I was like a candle in the process of extinction—my mental fire was going away in smoke. Through fidelity to a rule that was supposed to represent the will of God, I had forced myself to renounce all that was of real value in my working-class culture and education; and, since I could not assimilate the *bourgeois* education which was thrust upon me, there was very little of me left.'

The second evidence is from a twenty-year-old electrical fitter :

'I had to transform myself into a high-school boy, and gobble down in the shortest time possible all my secondary education. Everything I had done before entering was to be forgotten. I had to forget about my craft apprenticeship, and become a high-school boy and a *bourgeois*, so that I could acquire the gift of "pleasant and abundant" speech which, in theory, would make me a priest "for everyone". When I entered the seminary, I had to break with all my old friends, forget all that I had been, dissolve my personality, and pour it into the mould of the "classical" priesthood. At the beginning of my holidays I was told: "Don't fall back into your old environment". In spite of oneself, one is gradually transformed into another being.'

These two statements are quite sufficient to show how urgent it is that there should be a seminary adapted to the working-class, which will bring workers to the priesthood without overwhelming them with useless burdens. It was for this reason that Father Loew opened his training centre at Port-de-Bouc, and dedicated it to the protection of St. Peter (symbolizing the hierarchy) and St. Paul (symbolizing the mission).

At the beginning of 1963, Monsignor Ancel published a book called *Five Years with the Workers*, from which we have already quoted on several occasions in the course of this work. This was concerned with another experiment in the working-class apostolate, that of *Le Prado* at Lyons. Two secular priests, two religious, and a bishop led a working-class life from 1954 to 1959, in perfect obedience to the Roman directives. The author of the book was well aware that certain worker-priests thought differently from him on many points; but his argument is so delicately balanced, and he is so humble in his presentation, so careful to avoid giving offence, that it would be difficult for any opponent of his views to deny the truth of his human and spiritual insight.

In the first part of his book, Monsignor Ancel describes how he came to join a group of worker-priests: 'I must confess that I had been very reticent about the worker-priests; I did not believe that it was either necessary or possible for a priest to take on factory employment. I had not realized that such work could in fact be integrated into an entirely priestly way of life. . . . I did not feel at ease with the worker-priests, with their way of living, their way of speaking, their way of acting . . . gradually I was forced to admit that we no longer understood each other : and it was then, for the first time, that I had the idea of *going with them*. A comparison occurred to me : what would be thought of a vicar-apostolic, who resided in Paris, while his missionaries went to China?' (pp. 30-34.)

Monsignor Ancel, who was once a professor of philosophy, gives us his own analysis of the working-class character. He stresses the complexity of the working-class world : 'Reactions are different according to the size of the firm, and the skill of the worker; they are not the same at home as they are at work, they are not the same alone as they are in the group; they are not the same for someone living in a working-class area as they are for someone living in a mixed district'. (p. 116.) 'Among the working-class Communists, there are those who are workers-first, and those who are Communist-first. Many of those who vote Communist are in fact irritated by the "sectarians", and do not really want a Communist régime . . . still the vast majority do vote Communist, because there is no other party which is really capable of defending their interests.' (pp. 200-201.) 'Among the working-class there are unassimilated foreigners; and even among those you must learn to distinguish different categories—the Italians and the Spaniards, for instance, would not be in the same category as the Algerians. . . . You must learn to distinguish within the proletariat a subproletariat, and then within this subproletariat you have to make further distinctions. . . . There are the drunkards, and the ex-convicts, and various kinds of idler, some of them coming from quite different social circles. Then there is the upper fringe of petty artisans, small-scale traders, and men in positions of minor responsibility, whose reactions are sometimes very close to those of members of the working-class—though at other times you would think that they belonged to a completely different world. It is a bold man who claims that he knows the working-class well.' (pp. 118-119.)

Monsignor Ancel also points out the different influences which have contributed to the formation of the working-class mentality :

(1) *Socialism:* 'The working-class world is so profoundly influenced by the historical struggle in which it rose, and by socialist doctrines and their successive socialist leaders, that it is completely hardened against any form of capitalism, and can think only in socialist perspectives'. (p. 193.)

(2) *Marxism:* 'The Marxist class-struggle is understood in a fairly *simpliste* manner by the working-class. It is not bellicose by nature, but it is convinced that collaboration between workers and bosses is just out of the question. If anything is to be achieved, it must obviously be fought for'. (p. 186 and p. 198.)

(3) *Anti-religious rationalism:* 'Positively, this means the exaltation of man and his rights, in the spirit of nineteenth-century rationalism and the French Revolution; negatively, it means above all opposition to the Church'. (p. 202.)

(4) *Neo-materialism:* 'Household appliances and television sets have become the prime objects of working-class ambition. To achieve such goals in present economic conditions, which are still hard for most workers, it is necessary to work overtime or to do two jobs. The wife often has to work as well; hire-purchase agreements are made, and then sometimes they go short of food in order to meet repayments. These absorbing preoccupations have meant that a certain number of workers have allowed their personal ambition to overshadow their class-ambition—they have allowed their solidarity to be eaten away by a more or less

117

self-centred individualism. . . . The full results of this neo-materialism are still to be felt. . . . The militant workers are worried, and wonder whether it will lead to a serious degeneration.' (pp. 206-207.)

(5) *Christianity:* A certain number of Christian values survive. Action Catholique Ouvrière is beginning to have a distinct influence, but there is a general ignorance of the social doctrine of the Church. Monsignor Ancel enlarges on these themes, and says that he sometimes finds a deep and moving prayer in the hearts of the most violent anti-clericals. . . . We hear here the voice of a gentle pastor, putting us on our guard against rash judgements based on external data, which ignore the secret work of God in the depths of the soul.

Monsignor Ancel also makes observations on the working-class vocabulary, and way of reasoning. The vocabulary, he says, is poor and imprecise. Terms are used indiscriminately in senses appropriate now to one period of history, now to another; a pejorative sense is often given to words sacred to a Christian—such as 'charity'. Reasoning begins with facts, is inspired by emotion, and directed to action. It is a form of reasoning which is mainly a justification of intuition, and the intuition remains intact even when the reasoning is demolished by an opponent's 'theories'. . . . (pp. 120-144.)

In the second part of his book, Monsignor Ancel gives his pastoral reflections. He asks what the bible has to teach about the characteristics of a priest, God's messenger amongst men.

He does not think that it is *absolutely necessary* for a priest to work in order to be an apostle to the workers. He admits, however, that manual work is the *distinctive sign* of membership of this class. . . . The fact that a priest works with his hands is for the worker first of all a sign that he wishes to be really *present*—a friend, and a comrade. (pp.

262-3). His work also enables him to prove that he is not in the pay of 'the enemy'.

The two reasons which Monsignor Ancel finds to justify manual work have to do with the psychological impact on the workers; he does not, therefore, see the worker-priests in the same light as the Little Brothers of Jesus, for whom manual work is a value in itself, and an intrinsic part of the religious life.

Although he admits the usefulness and even the necessity of manual work for some working-class missionaries, he firmly rejects the idea that a priest should be 'temporally committed' : 'The worker-priest must not become a militant; this is not his work, it is not what he was sent to do', (p. 59); 'We would rather be misunderstood by our colleagues than accept work which is unfitting for us', (p. 91); 'There are two complementary aspects of the priest's refusal to accept temporal commitments; on the one hand, he has his own mission to accomplish; and, on the other hand, he must favour the promotion of laymen to their own proper responsibilities', (p. 270); 'Judging from our experience at Gerland, there is no doubt that this refusal does retard our identification with the working-class. If from the very beginning we had accepted positions of responsibility in the workers' organizations, we should have 'belonged' almost immediately; but this belonging would not have had its full symbolic value.' (p. 273). Monsignor Ancel recognizes that workers will not to begin with understand this position, any more than the Jewish people understood Jesus's refusal to be made King after the multiplication of the loaves; elsewhere, he says, 'We must not make this refusal a way of avoiding risks; we must search for kinds of commitment which are specifically evangelical', (p. 91.)

The experiment of Le Prado, as we can see, was guided by ideas similar to those of Father Loew. On the pastoral level, however, the two plans worked out in quite different ways. While Father Loew tried to formulate a large-scale project, Monsignor Ancel simply tried to find a place for his own work, side by side with the parish, side by side with Action Catholique, subject to them both, doing nothing without agreement, but asking simply that neither of them should consider itself the sole means of salvation, and deny to him his little place in the sun. (pp. 97, 329-353, 419-422, 440, etc.) In this we can sense his great concern to work together; and also the delicate regard he had for a whole range of susceptibilities, which he refused to brush aside.

In the third and last section, the author gives his views on the form which the interior life should take, not only of the worker-priests, but of all those dedicated to the mission to unbelievers. In these excellent pages, which are worthy of the most careful reading and meditation, we seem to be at a great spiritual meeting-place, where the thoughts of many modern apostles converge—of Father Chevrier, for instance, and Charles de Foucauld, who are mentioned explicitly, and also of Father Peyriguère, Abbé Huvelin, and of others who, under the guidance of the Holy Spirit, have drawn the same conclusions from their own interior lives and their apostolic experience.

This was the fruit of five years experience at Gerland—the experience of worker-priests, of worker-brothers, and of a worker-bishop.

Second Condemnation from the Holy Office

In June 1959, Cardinal Feltin was peruaded to draw up a report, in collaboration with other bishops, theologians, and ecclesiastical and lay organizations active among the working-class, on the various experiments made by the priests who had submitted to the hierarchy. The report was dated the 11th June 1959, and was accompanied by a request to Rome for permission to resume full-time work, provided certain conditions were fulfilled.

On the day *before* the publication of the report, however, the Holy Office held a convocation to consider the matter. A fortnight later, it gave its reply, in the negative, as in 1953. Through somebody's negligence, the memorandum from Rome to Cardinal Feltin announcing this decision got into the hands of the Press, and was immediately published in *Le Monde*. In this way the general public came to know the reasons used by the Holy Office to explain the suppression of the movement.

The Holy Office replied to the statistical evidence for the de-Christianization of the workers (at the port of Rouen, for instance, there was only one practising Catholic for every 700 workers, and in another section of industry 50 per cent are unbaptised), by taking a completely different point of view. 'It is hard to believe in the complete de-Christianization of masses of people of whom a very large number have received the indelible character of baptism'.

In spite of all the reasons urged by Father Loew and others in favour of undertaking factory work, the Holy Office put forward without any change the point of view which it held for twelve years : 'It is not essential to send priests as workers into the world of industrial labour. Despite all the efforts of recent years, and the experiments of the Little Brothers of Jesus, the Holy Office is compelled to pronounce that factory work is incompatible with the life and the obligations of the priesthood.'[2]

[2] It must be pointed out, however, that the information supplied to Rome by the Catholics of France was not always consistent. Some, for instance, stressed the survivals of Christianity which are to be found everywhere among the working-class; others drew attention to the magnificent results achieved by Action Catholique Ouvrière among the workers. It is not surprising that Rome arrived at this conclusion: 'However effective the worker-priests have been, it cannot be said that their presence is indispensible for the evangelization of the working class'.

Naturally, this decision provoked many responses. Here is a selection of them :

Cardinal Richaud: 'The letter does not say that manual work itself is incompatible with the priesthood, but only that certain conditions under which it is carried out in factories make it impossible for a priest to carry out his essential duties. Moreover, the letter does not refer to half-time employment'.

Cardinal Liénart: 'There is a profound de-Christianization in those areas of France which are entrusted to our care, particularly among the working-class. . . . It is the responsibility of bishops and priests first of all to bring the gospel to them'.

The entire French hierarchy: 'The mission of the worker-priests was carried out in conformity with the wishes of their bishops'.

An anonymous churchman in Le Monde, 25th September 1959 : 'A number of Catholics, Protestants, or even mere Christian sympathizers, seem to be astonished by the reactions to the decision of Rome; there are some who would find it quite natural that the priests who are more or less direct victims of this gross injustice or lack of understanding should rebel and leave the church.

'There is perhaps an error of perspective among the general public. It is obvious that there are scandals in the Roman Church. In particular, there has been a lasting malaise since the Vatican Council was interrupted in 1870, without reaching a clear definition of the *rôle* of the resident bishops with regard to the Papacy. It is certain aspects of this malaise which make the present situation peculiarly difficult, and it would be dishonest not to recognize this. There is, for instance, an astonishing incomprehension of the problems of France among certain dignitaries of the Church; we should ask what were the sources of information

122

which led them to this state of impermeability, and to this refusal to grant the French bishops the attention which they should rightly have.

'The thought of the Holy Office is remarkable for its sterilizing quality. Counsellors of a former generation, they cannot abide that anyone should disturb their vocabulary or their patterns of thought, which smack of rationalism rather than of theology. Such an attitude leads to a kind of unconscious pride, to an involvement in custom and tradition, which bears a striking similarity to the attitudes of the Sanhedrim. . . .

'Heavily under the influence of integralists, and in direct violation of the constitutive rules promulgated by Benedict XIV in the eighteenth century, the Holy Office today condemns without giving a hearing, openly refuses information which is not of the kind it desires to hear (quite apart from matters of faith), and often makes use of those very procedures which it condemns when they are practised by totalitarian states.

'Moreover, it is only too obvious that certain decisions, even over grave issues, are taken more in the light of personal and sectional rivalries than in the light of an objective study of the problems in hand.

'These criticisms are irrefutable, and people should know that we accept them without dissimulation, however painful this may be.

'Is this, however, a sufficient reason for revolt, for a rejection of the Catholic hierarchy, which forms an organic whole? To say so would be to forget elementary truths.

'In the first place, it is not in the least surprising that these men who live in their little worlds of libraries and offices should show signs of ordinary human weakness; those of us who live more simply than they still have a plentiful share of it! Entry into the machinery of a religious congregation

123

is no guarantee against deformation of character; we live in the real world and in real situations, not in some pious cloud-cuckoo land.

'But above all we must be clear about what we mean by the Church, and what we mean when we say "Rome". For us, the Church is a society both visibly and invisibly indissoluble. It is the assembly of all men of all ages redeemed in Christ; its expression in time, essential if we are not to lose contact, is the Catholic hierarchy—Pope and bishops—who continue by direct historical line the assembly of the first apostles. For us, there can be no question of separating the two aspects of this one perfect and definitive society, at once temporal and eternal.

'In this immense organic whole, which St. Paul calls the mystical body, the Holy Office represents only one necessary member. The Holy Office is not the Church, it is merely an organ of government; but it cannot be dissociated from the Church. If it functions well, so much the better; if it functions badly, so much the worse—it must still be supported. The Church is a living body; the toe would not cut itself off from the body because the stomach had pains—it must wait until the stomach gets over its pains. It is nonsense to talk about revolting against the Church on the pretext that the Holy Office or some other organ does not satisfy us in its visible functions; we simply have to wait until the Church has digested its follies.

'The public on the other hand, encouraged by certain organs of the Press, tends to confuse the issues. When such and such a prelate expresses a debatable or a foolish opinion, there is a tendency to report it as what *Rome* thinks; but a Roman is not Rome, nor is he necessarily immune from stupidity.

What is thought *at* Rome, however, is not what the Church thinks either. The most striking proof of this is that

Pope John XXIII decided to convoke an ecumenical council—a move which could not have delighted the hearts of certain "Romans" who were beginning to lose sight of the Church. . . .

'It would be short-sighted to revolt, even in the face of unacceptable incidents; it would show a purely temporal, political, and non-religious view of the Church.

'It would also be very dangerous. For when certain "rabbinical" factions, whether Jansenist or integralist, have succeeded in procuring a condemnation of those who wish to work in a more vital way, they are only too delighted to see the "condemned" in revolt. Can they not then say, "We told you so—see how the wolves have come out of their sheep's clothing!" The triumph of the Rabbis, the Jansenists, or the Integralists is complete—and, apparently, legitimate. If Father Lagrange had revolted against the decisions of the biblical commission, we should still be waiting for that extraordinary renewal of scripture scholarship which is a beacon light of our time.

'When we, anonymous priests of France, see our colleagues in the public eye made the victims of flagrant injustice, a reflex of sympathy and indignation impels us towards revolt, and the full expression of our disgust. But this is only a passing phase. We then make the effort to see further than the immediate and apparent situation.

'Certain individuals highly placed in the Roman congregations should know, however, that, though we obey, we are not deceived. We obey the living mystery of the Church, of which they are a part, but which transcends them infinitely—the Church of which they know only one aspect. The persistence and vitality of this Church in spite of such obstacles is an enduring miracle; in the logic of our faith alone can we pray for those responsible for these decisions.'

On the next day, a priest of the Society of Jesus wrote to *Le Monde* : 'In the name of the clergy of our parish, I wish to express the immense satisfaction with which we read yesterday's article on "The Holy Office and the Church". It expressed in a clear and vigorous manner, though sometimes rather too aggressively, sentiments which we share, and which we believe are common to a large part of the French clergy. It was a tremendous release to see them in print. Instead of the spate of articles expressing pious benedictions, resignation, or revolt, it is vital to emphasize at once the deficiencies of the Roman machinery, and our absolute, lucid, though often painful attachment to Church hierarchical, spiritual, and Roman.

'We are privileged to live at a time when we can base this attachment, not on ignorance or fear, but on the rigorous demands of faith and reason. This body of the Church, which is ours, is sick; we understand better the cause of its illness; but it is still our body, and through it life comes to us. We shall work with obstinate patience, and with an even more rigorous sincerity (to counteract the "ecclesiastical lies"), to make this body in all its members and in all its functioning a more faithful expression of the Spirit which lives within it and guides it. In this we show our fidelity both to Christ and to the men of our time.'

Three weeks later, M. Latreille, professor at the University of Lyons, and a former director of public worship in the Ministry of the Interior, wrote as follows : 'In the light of a prolonged study of ecclesiastical history, I should like to add the following remarks to the reflections published in *Le Monde* :

(1) It is correct to say that the Roman Curia cannot claim to be the well-informed government which we sometimes like to imagine. In many cases, Rome is ill-informed of the

concrete problems facing the faithful; and for this there are two reasons :

(a) because it is an absolute government, accustomed to a hasty approbation of all its intentions, and its dignitaries are often ready to take offence at anything which resembles an expression of disagreement; consequently, it takes no steps to collect independent witnesses who could help to establish the facts.

(b) because the objections which do reach it only come by way of diplomats, who are obliged, not to distort, but to 'pad' their ideas. Anyone who has had anything to do with the correspondence between Papal Nuncios and the Secretary of State knows with what circumlocutions even the boldest spirits present facts which might be supposed disagreeable to the Supreme Pontiff.

(2) If the government of the Church is not well-informed concerning the mentality of groups to which it is a stranger, or whose loyalty is suspect, (if only because of their frankness), it has, on the other hand a great advantage over secular governments in that :

(a) it has a much larger horizon, which enables it to consider problems in the perspective of a universal and super-temporal society (The Church).

(b) it can envisage problems less in terms of expediency or movements of opinion, and more in terms of their specifically religious meaning.

(c) it can take time to reflect, with that grave sense of responsibility which it has, on the events which are reported to it.

Because of this, the Holy See has succeeded, thanks to a spiritual sense which it has seldom lacked, and to an unequalled experience of human nature, in accurately discerning the risk of error in certain intellectual attitudes, or the risk to ecclesiastical discipline in certain practices, even when the judgements of its courts have been formed on very inadequate grounds.

(3) The more a government is convinced that its actions are well-adapted to achieve its purposes, the more those who carry responsibility in it will be attached to those methods which they consider have stood the test of time. This is particularly true of the Roman Curia, since no one is allowed to point out to it the pastoral inconveniences of the methods it employs.

This certainty of being right could, however, and perhaps should, be a permanent invitation to reform these methods, to take into account the difficulties sometimes caused by 'injunctions,' and to respect the legitimate aspirations of the conscience of the people.

The following changes appear to be desirable :

(a) As your correspondent suggests, there should be a reform in the methods of enquiry employed by the Holy Office, on the lines laid down by Pope Benedict XIV. These methods are not only out-of-date—that in itself would not be important—but they show too little respect for the dignity of the person, which the Church sets out to defend on every possible occasion in the modern world;

(b) The Catholic Press and the Catholic public should cease to regard every loyal proposal on this difficult subject as a crime of pontifical *lèse-majesté*, or as some dreadful aspect of modernism.'

At this time Father Loew wrote to his friends a confidential letter, full of sorrow but without bitterness, and still confident and respectful with regard to the authority of the Church. We take the liberty now to quote the conclusion of this 'strictly personal' letter :

'For this year, I shall try to follow the advice the Curé d'Ars gave to an author : "Instead of making a clamour in

128

the Press, you would do better to make a clamour at the doors of the Tabernacle".'

At the beginning of March 1960, Pope John XXIII, moved by the obedience of the former worker-priests, expressed his satisfaction with them, and congratulated Cardinal Feltin on his conduct of the affair.

Can we foresee the future of the worker-priests experiment? Only to the limited extent that the future is always the fruit of the past.

The past has evoked in the Roman authority certain apprehensions and certain decisions which are bound to have an influence on the future; some doors may open, but some are definitely closed. The present position of the Holy Office can be summarised as follows:

(1) *The traditional conception of the priesthood cannot be sacrificed.*

It is the conception of the *priesthood* rather than the question of the pastoral ministry, or of the missions, or of the apostolate, which must be retained; this means the mass, public prayer, the distribution of the sacraments and the preaching of the Word. 'All the other activities of the priest must be in some way subordinated to these functions, and must derive from them as practical consequences.'

(a) There are two points to notice here. The Holy Office does not require every priest to fulfil *all the priestly functions*. Monks do not administer the sacraments, and seldom preach. The same is true of a number of priest-teachers. But the worker-priests must have *some* specifically priestly function, whether it is in the domain of preaching (in one form or another), or of the sacraments, or of prayer.

(b) The worker-priest will have to re-think his presence in the factory and the neighbourhood, and his manual work,

in order to see how they can become activities ordained in some way by his priestly character, and 'deriving from it as a practical consequence'.

Father Loew and Monsignor Ancel have already thought to some purpose along these lines.

(2) *Everything which is incompatible with the activities of the priest, directly or indirectly, must be excluded from his life.*

This does not mean, evidently, that manual work must be excluded, since the Trappists have always regarded this as part of their religious lives. The Holy Office has in mind specifically *factory-work*; and this for two reasons:

(a) This work takes too much time and energy and does not leave sufficient time to fulfil the priestly functions which we have just described.

We are certainly all in agreement that an intense interior life is essential for worker-priests, and that they must therefore have a form of life which adapted to this need. This interior life is the foundation not only of their priesthood, but of their apostolate; on this point the third part of Monsignor Ancel's book, which deals with the doctrine of pre-mission, is of capital importance. The interior life of the apostle is his first missionary activity, which conditions all the others.

(b) The Holy Office is also seriously concerned about the factory environment; it considers that the atmosphere which it engenders is such that those who work in it must necessarily fall under the influence of Marxism and materialism.

It is of course true that the large factory in particular is a very bad environment. Monsignor Ancel however raises a difficulty which cannot be avoided: 'If the factory environment is dangerous for the spiritual life and the chastity of priests, and if the fact of living in this environment leads

130

the workers necessarily to Marxism, has a *Christian of any kind* the right to work in a factory, or even in small industrial undertakings?' (op. cit., p. 459.)

Today members of certain religious congregations and members of secular institutes have in fact the right to work full-time in factories; if their experience is favourable, perhaps the Holy Office will gain confidence, and permit the priests to join them.

(3) *The worker-priests 'devote to manual work time which should be given to the priestly ministry or to religious studies'.*

Yet a great number of priests are permitted to devote their priestly lives to the teaching of profane sciences. The authorities consider that this teaching can be the means of handing on a Christian orientation, and that a priest must be a teacher to do this. The workers however absorb many of their ideas in the factory, and these ideas also must be given a Christian orientation; and since a priest can only be present in the factory at the workers' own level by himself being a worker, it is possible that, as the other objections fall, this last one may also be removed.

Prophecy is rash; but insofar as the past can throw light on the future, these are the lines of development which seem possible in the years to come.

CHAPTER V

The Problems Which Remain

THE CONFLICT over the worker-priests drew attention to a divergence of attitudes which has existed in the Church from the times of the apostles; it is the same divergence, basically, which divides St. James from St. Paul, and which is echoed in the Acts and the Epistles. It is a divergence which will no doubt continue to exist until the Last Day. It can hardly be expected, therefore, that the suppression of the worker-priests will eliminate the conflict, or remove the mutual incomprehension. The fundamental problem remains what it always was: the confrontation of two opposed mentalities, of two spiritualities, of two different conceptions of the apostolate.

(1)   *Two mentalities: the Right and the Left*[1]

Order consists in a balance of reciprocal rights and duties, and is a necessity for any society. The duty of authority is to establish this order.

Unfortunately, authority does not always carry out its function; the 'order' which it maintains can easily become a kind of disorder—a system of legalized injustice. The

[1] Political parties classify themselves, rightly or wrongly, as 'Right' and 'Left'. This discussion is not meant to have any direct relevance to such alignments, but is merely concerned with the basic psychology of the two points of view.

psalmist speaks of the 'Throne of Iniquity' which 'frameth mischief by the law'. (Psalm xciv. 20.)

From this there arises a conflict of conscience in which everyone is bound to take sides—either for authority, or for justice. Goethe takes one attitude : 'Better an injustice than disorder'—this is the view of the Right. Morvan Lebèque takes the other, when he says that there can only be 'order' where there is justice. He speaks for the men of the Left.

It would be untrue, however, to say that the Right is 'for' order, whereas the Left is 'against' order. They are both for order. For the Right, order is the fruit of obedience; for the Left, it is the fruit of justice.

The men of the Right think that authority alone should resolve problems of conscience; the subordinate has only to obey.

In defence of their attitude, the men of the Right are accustomed to refer to various scriptural texts :

Titus iii. 1 : 'Admonish them to be subject to princes and powers'.

1 Peter ii. 18 : 'Servants, be subject to your masters with all fear, not only when they are kind and considerate, but even when they are perverse'.

Ephesians vi. 5-7 : 'Slaves, obey your earthly masters with fear and trembling, singlemindedly, as serving Christ. . . . Give the cheerful service of those who serve the Lord, not men.'

Romans xiii. 1-5 : 'Every person must submit to the supreme authorities. There is no authority but by act of God, and the existing authorities are instituted by Him; consequently, anyone who rebels against authority is resisting a divine institution, and those who so resist shall have themselves to thank for the punishment they receive.'

Hebrews xiii. 17 : 'Obey your leaders and defer to them'.

They also quote in their support the words of Jesus :

133

'Whoever listens to you, listens to me; and whoever despises you, despises me'. (Luke x. 16.) They apply these words to all orders emanating from any authority—regardless of the fact that they only refer, in their original context, to the preaching of the gospel. When it comes to the question of directing consciences, the men of the Right insist on complete self-exposure, and complete obedience. Their reasoning is as follows: those in authority have received a special grace—God gives them the light which they need in order to direct you, and they see further than you can see. 'Our Lord may well be glorified more by your obedience than by all the good you can do'. (St. Vincent de Paul.) 'One diamond is worth more than a mountain of stones; one act of virtuous submission more than a mountain of good works done for others. We must consider that we are always doing the will of God when we do the will of our superiors, and that we tread the path of chaos and disorder when we do otherwise.'

The Right is therefore distrustful of the initiatives of subordinates. Perfection is to be sought in obedience. St. Vincent de Paul wrote, 'You must conform in all things with the rules and customs of the Congregation. Introduce nothing new, but respect the opinions of those who are in charge of the houses of the order. . . . We should abandon ourselves to the Providence of God, and should not try to overtake it. . . . Our custom has always been to wait for orders from above, not to anticipate them.'

This attitude leads to an obsequious and equivocal veneration of 'Superiors'. The Pope becomes the 'visible Christ', the priest 'another Christ'; titles are multiplied— Reverend, Reverend Father, *Reverendissime,* etc. etc. Genuflections are the order of the day. John XXIII is reported as saying, 'I am *not* His Holiness, I'm just the Pope, that's all . . . one genuflection a day is quite enough!'

In every situation, the man of the Right will have the same spontaneous reaction: the voice of authority must always be obeyed and respected.

The Left also quotes scripture in its favour:

Acts iv. 19 records an occasion on which St. Peter himself refused obedience to the Jewish authorities: 'Is it right in God's eyes for us to obey you rather than God? Judge for yourselves'. St. John also has a warning: 'Do not trust any and every spirit; test the spirits, to see whether they are from God, for among those who have gone out into the world there are many prophets falsely inspired'. (1 John iv. 1.)

The Old Testament supplies similar material: 'Forasmuch therefore as thou hast rejected the word of the Lord, the Lord hath also rejected thee from being king'. (1 Sam. xv. 23.)

The Left can also invoke in its support a number of philosophical doctrines concerning power and personal responsibility. St. Thomas Aquinas, though naturally favouring monarchy rather than democracy, teaches that the power which comes from God is deposited first of all with the people, who have the right to delegate it to those who must exercise it. All human obedience is therefore conditioned by an overriding principle which everyone recognizes, at least in theory: 'We must obey God rather than men'. (Acts v. 29.)

Teilhard de Chardin wrote in *Energie Spirituel de la Souffrance*: 'True obedience sometimes consists in marching north, when superiors order a march to the south or the west'.

The Left cannot see why an individual should have been given his intelligence in order not to use it or his will in order to let other people do his deciding for him. 'We in the West know that the supreme worth of a man lies in the autonomy of his conscience, in that sovereign independence which enables an indvidual to transform the circumstances in which he finds himself, to break an old pattern by a movement of the Spirit, to make it conform more truly with a vision of Truth and Justice. This we call liberty'. (P. H. Simon.)

If this is a dangerous position, it is nevertheless a position supported by the highest authority; on the 3rd October 1953 Pius XII said : 'No authority has a right to command an immoral act; there can be no right, obligation, or permission to carry out an act which is intrinsically immoral, even when such an act is commanded, and when a refusal to obey could involve great personal peril'.

The man of the Left therefore does not refuse obedience itself; what he refuses is blind obedience, and obedience in injustice. He cannot renounce his personal responsibility by obeying orders; for him, an authentic act of obedience must be an act which is willed and understood.

The man of the Left may be proud; but in justice we must acknowledge that his attitude is often nearer to heroism than to cowardice. He feels instinctively responsible for his acts, and he has a urgent and demanding sense of justice. This makes him all the more aware of the human weakness, the limitations and the deficiencies of those in authority; he cannot stand by while human authority usurps the rights of God.

Perhaps these brief observations will be sufficient to bring to mind the two mentalities which confronted each other in the worker-priest conflict, as they have done in all the major conflicts of the past, and as they will continue to do in the conflicts of the future.

(2) *Two views of authority*

The authoritarian superior prefers to rule alone. He avoids consulting the views of his subordinates, or, if he is

forced to do so, he does not really take them into account.
He keeps his distance, and issues orders. If he is in charge
of a large organization, he often makes use of a kind of
intelligence department to ensure that his directives are
carried out. He can often appear as a benevolent dictator;
he has a lively sense of his own responsibility, and of his
own dignity, and does not doubt for a moment that the
orders which he gives come directly from the Holy Spirit.
He writes with confidence at the head of all his decisions
In Nomine Domini. If he is criticized for his faults or his
omissions, he is inclined to suspect his critic of the crime of
lèse-majesté, in questioning the prerogatives of the Almighty.
Sometimes his very sense of humanity becomes dulled by
his pre-occupation with the divine.

The superior of the collegiate type, on the other hand,
is concerned above all to form a team with his subordinates.
His position is for him a position of service and of ministry,
not a position of dignity. He also believes in the Holy Spirit,
but he believes that this Spirit can enlighten all men of
goodwill, and that consequently an inconspicuous subordinate can often instruct the wisest leaders. 'To be a
member of a team', wrote Abbé Michonneau, 'we must will
together, think together, work together, progress together;
we must commit ourselves together, and learn together from
our trials.' Father Loew considered himself *primus inter
pares* in his team, the first among equals, the elder brother
of the family.

This attitude, which is manifestly more rewarding and
more balanced than the former, is nevertheless more
dangerous for 'order'. It presupposes a superior who can
be both humble and firm, with subordinates who have
escaped from the snares of individualism. We could hardly
call those young curates good 'team-members', for instance,
who reduced the role of their Parish-priests to three simple

rules—to listen to them (and not interfere in discussions), to serve them (and do the work they did not want to do), and to cover them with the authorities!

The men of the Left who claim to think for themselves are obviously difficult subjects to direct. Their obedience is founded on the principle of dialogue; and at the end of every dialogue, they reserve the right, in all conscience, to disobey.

During the history of the worker-priests, there was much stupidity, much childishness, much to regret . . . but behind all this was an incessant conflict between a Rightist authority, which demanded unconditional submission, and the natural Leftist temperament of the worker-priests, who longed for genuine dialogue.[2]

Their attitude was variously appreciated. *Documentation Catholique* (21st March 1954) recorded: 'This dangerous spirit of independence with regard to the hierarchy is the result of their conviction that no useful directive can come from superiors who have no experience of the proletariat'. *Actualité Religieuse* (October 1953) took a slightly different

---

[2] The worker-priests also had to cope at this time with a number of seductive invitations. On the 23rd February 1954, for instance, the periodical *Franc-Tireur* published this:

'The people of France are following with interest the polemical debate between the worker-priests and the Holy Office. The worker-priests who wish to continue their mission, but at the same time are not willing to leave their priestly callings, may not be aware of the existence of a vigorous Old Catholic Gallican Apostolic Church (in the tradition of Bossuet). They are at liberty to write to His Holiness the Patriarch of the Gallican Church (9 bis, Rue Jean-de-Beauvais, Paris Vième), who replies to all letters, welcomes with paternal benevolence all wounded souls, and gives them the means of continuing their ministry.'

It is true that some of the worker-priests demanded to be reduced to the lay state, and others begged this right without demanding it; but at the same time they evidently preferred this agonizing solution to compromising themselves by joining a schismatic church. Even in this they were responsive to the Holy Spirit.

view: 'If ever the Roman authorities consider it necessary
to resort to extreme measures, let them at least indicate
clearly what was wrong with the experiment, and what
caused its failure. Those who fought so hard have a right at
least to the honours of war. . . . No one questions the
authority which comes from above; but the worker-priests
should surely be allowed, by the grace of Mother Church,
the mistress of truth, to make their own self-criticism; they
have learnt from their colleagues in the factories how to
call a spade a spade.'

Father Finet summed up: 'Whether we like it or not,
there are two opposed mentalities in conflict; and it is far
too easy a solution to say that one truly represents Jesus
Christ, and the other is in error'.

The Left-Right divergence is found in the clergy and the
hierarchy as well as in the laity. In his study *Catholicism
Today*, Joseph Folliet wrote: 'On the social level, Marxists
and some Christians maintain that the Church is bound to
capitalism and the *bourgeoisie*; this view is not just a sim-
plification, it is a falsification, as can be proved by any
serious investigation'. He reminds us, quite rightly, that in
the upper *bourgeoisie* of business and finance there are
more protestants, Jews, and non-religious than there are
Catholics. Rockefeller was not a Catholic, nor was Henry
Deterding, Carnegie, Pierpont-Morgan, Bazil Zaharov,
Krupps or Rothschild, who have each reigned over a large
sector of industry during the last half-century. All the same,
quite a number of large industrialists do belong to the
Church. In the countries which remained Catholic at the
Reformation, it is the *bourgeoisie* of the senior military and
civilians officials, the landed *bourgeoisie* mixed with the old
aristocracy, the higher technicians and the directors of large
public and private enterprises, the intellectuals and the
members of the liberal professions who constitute the vast

majority of those we call 'practising Catholics'. This social group, by origin, temperament, education, social position or mere self-interest can be broadly classified as belonging to the Right.

'The worker-priests asked themselves and their superiors questions which profoundly disturbed the interests of big capital, of which the Catholic hierarchy is a faithful guardian.'

This statement from *Humanité* (17th September 1953) could be an exaggeration; but the following article published in *Le Monde* (March 1952) cannot be so easily dismissed:

'Certain persons who have on their lips incessantly condemnations, decrees, cautions, and other arguments from authority, easily win a reputation for orthodoxy and fidelity. Their method is denunciation and calumny. They swarm in the antechambers of the Vatican, in the corridors of the *Chambre des Députés*, and cloak their political aims with doctrinal purity. Much of this kind of rubbish has issued from the journals of the extreme Right, which today, as always, sets out to school the Church, the bishops, and all that is living in French Catholicism with their sterile morality.

'Meanwhile, other interests, more hidden but more effective, draw profit from this campaign. Bishops are graciously watered with an abundance of rightist literature; tracts printed and circulated throughout the presbyteries of the country. Someone provides the money; not, we may assume, without a reason. . . .'

Cardinal Feltin himself declared before an international conference of Catholic Charities that 'the Vatican was insufficiently informed of what was of real value in the worker-priest experiment, because of its reliance on one-sided and negative reports'.

It is hard for ecclesiastical authority to escape from the

influence of the Christian *milieu* which surrounds it, advises it (directly or indirectly), and supports its existence. Obviously, this authority cannot remain indifferent to the attitudes of its practising members—this would be a betrayal of its mission. That is why the Church is slow to reform. The laity may have a modest position in the official hierarchy, but they are not without influence on the powers that be.

The Church is a mystical body; but it is also a visible society. 'As it exists in the world, it has heavy responsibilities —schools, hospitals, charities, missions, ceremonies. To meet these responsibilities, it needs considerable financial resources. It would be strange if this subservience did not give a certain direction to some of its thinking.

'This is a grave matter in which we must all take our share of responsibility. The scandal caused to those who were beginning to regard the Church with friendship and confidence is already so great that it is hard to see how it can be remedied. "When we tell them that the decisions which have been taken were not political ones, they say that we have ourselves been taken in—that we are treating them like imbeciles, and losing contact altogether with reality." (Témoignage Chrétien, 19th February 1954.)

'Father Ducos's assertion that the Church is not an ally of capitalism will only convince those who want to be convinced, those who are ill-informed. It is common knowledge that the Vatican is one of the world's most important financial powers, if not the most important. Through its controlling interest in numerous industrial, commercial and banking organizations it forms an integral part of the capitalist system. It could hardly hope for the disappearance of the system from which it draws profit. It will take more than a few thousand priests like Father Ducos to whitewash the capitalist hierarchy of the Catholic Church.

141

The Church simply uses their disinterested labours for its own propagandist ends—they help to build up its alibis, its moral refuge against the winds of criticism. With the best intentions in the world, these priests only help to maintain an appearance of ambiguity—if anyone is foolish enough to be taken in by them.' (*Express*, 23rd December 1959.)

There are various way of meeting this attack. We may think of Bergson's meditation on the humility of God. When the Son of God took to Himself a human body, He began to walk in the way of humiliation; this was the mystery of Christmas. When he dragged his battered body up the hill of Calvary, he humbled Himself still further; this was the mystery of Good Friday. It was an even greater humiliation when He took a worthless and lifeless piece of bread, and said, 'This is my Body'—and this was the mystery of Maundy Thursday. The final humiliation, however, was when Christ united Himself to His social and mystical body, to a body covered with sins and overcome with weakness, filthy from its labours among the factories and rubbish-heaps of the world; this was the ultimate scandal, the mystery of Pentecost.

This body nailed on the cross is His own body, and so is the Body of the Church, which we constitute. He foresaw the humiliation of His social body, the Church, just as He foresaw the humiliation of His physical body; and he accepted them both. We cannot think about the weakness of the Church, without at the same time thinking of the humility of God; the two themes are bound together by the union of Christ with His Church that St. Paul speaks of— a mystery which should put us on our guard against rash criticism, for in attacking one we may harm the other.

The way to show a real concern about the authenticity and the sanctity of the Church, is to do something which will help to realize it. 'The real scandal', wrote Etienne Borne, 'for those who have any spiritual perception, is that a religion destined for the whole of mankind should become static and confined in a closed institutional Christianity, incorporated with the feudal world, with the *bourgeoisie*, with Western civilization, turning a deaf ear to the barbarian hordes who batter uncouthly at its prudently bolted doors'. (*Carrefour*, 23rd September 1953.) Those who hear the clamour which the others ignore must remain within the Church for that very reason. God gives them the grace of good hearing—a grace entrusted to them, as St. Paul puts it, for the edification of the Church.

We stay because there is work to do; we stay because there is too much of human and supernatural value in the Church for it to be adandoned because of a conflict of mentalities.

'Just as the appearance of men is affected by their geographical environment, as with the men of the desert, the men of the frozen North, the sad and nervous men of the great cities, so the appearance of the Church is affected by its historical environment. The complaint is sometimes heard that in order to be at ease in the Church one has to have a feudal mentality.' (*Combat*, 5th December 1953.) Certainly the feudal epoch left a profound impression on the appearance of the Church; but the modern world also will leave its impression. In spite of all the obstruction of narrow traditionalists, everything of value which we can fashion will be sooner or later assumed by the Church. It is for this reason that we must work, and hope—in order that we should not have to leave.

(3) *Two forms of spirituality: flight, and incarnation*
(a) Flight. The 'spirituality of flight' dates back to the time of the first hermits, in the period of peace which followed the heroic strife of the first three centuries and the

143

years of persecution; or we may trace its origins even further back, to the community of Qumran in the time of Christ, or even to the prophet Elias, whom the Carmelites claim as their founder, in the ninth century B.C.

Life in the world is a tissue of compromise between the spirit and the flesh. Whether we like it or not, we are obliged to betray, to lie, to steal, to prostitute our talents. It is not surprising that some Christians prefer to 'leave the world', and cut themselves off in solitude to remain loyal to the experiences of faith. Is this an easy way out?—or is it rather a sovereign assertion of independence with regard to the world?

Unfortunately, the men who leave the world are still men. Without the constraint of life in society, some hermits gave way to boredom, negligence, and evil fantasies.

St. Basil in the East, and St. Benedict in the West, worked out a new formula which would enable people to withdraw from the world, but would at the same time avoid the anarchy of solitude. They proposed a communal life, regulated by a rule and controlled by a superior. Obedience to the rule is hard, especially as it co-ordinates all activity at every hour of the day and night. There is no place left for personal whims, and the life is one of constant renunciation. It is also visualized as a battle—a battle against the devil who follows us everywhere, and a battle against ourselves. Bernanos said that sanctity was an adventure—'The only real adventure there is'.

It is also a life of work. The contemplative orders insisted on eight hours work a day, as well as eight hours prayer. These men who fled from the world were certainly not parasites or idlers—there is many a housewife, many an official, many a businessman, who works much less than they. We have only to think of the part played by the abbeys in the formation of our civilization, and their life-giving influence during the desolate years which followed the decline of Rome.

The centuries passed, but Christian spirituality continued in the same direction. The monastic ideal, perfectly valid within the abbey, gradually invaded the whole of Christian spirituality. Eventually, it was no longer possible to think of a 'life of perfection' except as an 'escape from the world'.

Occasionally saints tried to work out something new, but their experiments were abortive. St. Francis's idea of founding 'little groups of joyful brothers living simply according to the gospels' had a dubious reception from Innocent III; how could there be an authentic religious life outside the monastery? The Franciscan rule which was eventually approved by Honorius III did not quite correspond with the dream of St. Francis. . . . Three hundred years later, St. Francis of Sales also had his dream of a community of religious who would leave the seclusion of the cloister and go into the world to devote themselves to the needy. Once more, traditionalist opinion was scandalized; evangelical charity was not enough. The *visitandines* of St. Francis of Sales remained in the cloister, like their elder sisters.

At the time of the Renaissance, societies of priests were founded, dedicated to the ministry of the people, but living in communities, and following a rule under the direction of a superior. Among them were the Barnabites, the Redemptorists, and the Passionists. Their conception of the religious life was basically monastic; and, since many of them founded seminaries, it is not surprising that they communicated to the parish clergy their own spirituality of flight.

This influenced the idea of 'priestly prayer'. An enormous number of spiritual exercises were imposed. Each day: a meditation, spiritual reading, rosary, a visit to the Blessed Sacrament; each week: the Way of the Cross, and Confession; each month: a period of recollection. Regular spiritual direction, and examination of conscience twice a day. On top of all this, daily mass—the priestly prayer *par excellence*—and recitation of the very long monastic prayers of the divine office. Thus, ever since the counter-Reformation, the secular priest has been bound to a life of prayer at least as extensive as that of a monk.

After all these acts of devotion, the priest's own truly pastoral prayer can begin: the administration of the sacraments (baptisms, confessions, marriages, anointing of the sick), burials, the preaching of the Word, etc.

The Holy Office showed a legitimate concern; how indeed could the worker-priests, on top of his day's work at the factory, carry out all these exercises of devotion? Already our urban clergy have to perform spiritual acrobatics— such as reading their breviary while presiding at a burial —and even then, of course, they don't always succeed.

The spirit of this life of prayer is equally characteristic of its monastic origins. Prayer is often presented in the seminaries (though less often now than in the past) as a flight, not only from the world, but even from pastoral work. The attitude may not be general, but it is significant. The secular priest is looked upon as a kind of monk, who has to be sacrificed to the needs of Christians in the world, but feels all the time a nostalgia for the cloister. This is the ideal which still haunts us—and with it belongs the old idea of the priest who fails to achieve his own salvation while realizing that of others.

The 'spirituality of flight' also leaves its impression on the so-called 'priestly virtues'.

The first of these is *obedience*—obedience to the rule. The 'rule' is conceived in monastic terms, and the seminary becomes a kind of prolonged novitiate; the rule takes care of everything. In one such seminary, until a few years ago,

146

hair-cuts were regulated, leather soles were prohibited, cigarettes and cigars permitted but not pipes, etc. etc.[3] The ideal of the seminarian was to do the will of God; but the will of God meant 'the rule'.

Breaches of the rule, which to outsiders would seem quite trivial (such as smoking four times a week instead of three) often involved expulsion from the seminary, without any chance of entering in another diocese. This rigidity was justified by the following argument :

The seminarian who obeys the rule today will tomorrow, when he is a curate or a teacher, be a docile instrument in the hands of his parish priest or his director; he will easily put aside appeals from outside, or initiatives of his own choice. The obedience of the priest is conceived in the same terms as the obedience of the monk.

Another virtue frequently praised is *chastity*.

It is to be expected that a priest should have a great esteem for celibacy, a state to which he is called both for practical and for spiritual reasons. But chastity can take various colourings, according to its context. St. Gregory of Nyssa, for example, considered that Adam and Eve had suffered a double punishment for their sin; namely, corruptibility, and procreation by means of sexual intercourse. Marriage was given to them as a consolation for death. The end of the Christian life should be to return to the lost paradise; and the first thing to abandon is marriage. Celibacy is the first step which leads back to God. This is chastity conceived as a virtue of flight.[4]

Nowadays, psychologists insist habitually on the difference between repression of desire, which involves frustration and tension, and true *virtue* (virtus), which is the transformation of desire and the self-mastery that bring joy, love, and

---

[3] These details are quite accurate. The regulations applied until 1945.
[4] *Platonisme et Théologie Mystique*, Daniélou, pp. 85ff.

fulfilment. The distinction is vital; it is in this light that we should understand the teaching of St. Bernard: 'Virginity merits a reward, but humility is also necessary. You can be saved without chastity, but not without humility. God can take into His grace the humble who weep over their lost virginity, but without humility, even the virginity of Mary would not have pleased Him. If therefore you can only admire the virginity of Mary, be content to imitate her humility; that is enough for you.'[5] The celibacy which the Church rightly asks of her priests is only of real value in Christian and human terms if it is founded on true *virtue* (not on repression), and on humility (not on hardened pride).

The last of the classical virtues is *dignity*. The high esteem in which the priest is held must be accompanied by an external dignity, and a certain distance with regard to other men. The priest must inspire respect by his dress, his manners, his speech, and by the place he lives in. He must remain a man apart—*segregatus a populo*; all that he says, and all that he does, must carry a stamp of gravity—*nihil nisi grave*. This distance from others is in addition a safeguard for his chastity.

This is more or less the ideal of the diocesan priest as it has developed since the counter-Reformation. It is marked in every aspect by the spirituality of flight. It has had its moments of historical glory; it was in this school that the priesthood learned to drag itself out of the mire of the renaissance, and to recognize fully certain priestly virtues which in one form of another will always be indispensable. It is doubtful however whether such a spirituality can meet all the needs of the modern apostolate.

The point of view of such a spirituality, a movement like that of the worker-priests, even when surrounded by the most elaborate precautions, will always be unacceptable.

[5] First homily of St. Bernard on the Praise of the Virgin Mary.

(b) The Spirituality of Incarnation. Side by side with the spirituality of flight, there is throughout the tradition of the Church a contrary tendency, a quest of sanctity within the world, sanctity for those who work and live with other men—a spirituality of incarnation. This movement belongs first of all with the laity, and must be studied closely in Catholic Action movements (concerned with the revaluation of professional work, the Christian vision of social structures, etc.) and in the domain of marriage (consider for example the work done by the *Equipes de Notre-Dame, Groupes de Ménage*), etc.

Incarnational spirituality must however also be the concern of priests whose lives are dedicated to pastoral work. The priest too must find his human and priestly fulfilment in his work, in his pastoral mission, and his spiritual food must be first of all his own pastoral prayer—the mass, the administration of the sacraments, the preaching of the word, etc. This spirituality, which is booming now, is marked off from the other by a number of contrary options:

(c) Primacy of the gospel over the rule. A young father of a family had been ill in bed for nearly ten years. His case was taken over by a great doctor who, after thirty years research, thought that he had found a cure for the sick man's complaint. In order to convince the patient, he gave him the name and address of a religious who had been suffering from the same disease, and who had regained the use of his limbs. His new hope half-stifled by distrust, the young man wrote immediately to the religious to find out all that he could. And his reply? A polite note from the superior, reminding him that it was now the Lenten season, and that the Holy Rule 'did not permit the sisters to engage in correspondence during the period of penance'.

According to the spirituality of incarnation, such a decision is stupid, and contrary to the most elementary

149

laws of charity. Yet the superior was no doubt convinced that her decision was the best for everyone—for herself, because she was doing her duty with regard to the rule; and for the sick man, because he was being given the opportunity to offer to God a salutary sacrifice, an exercise of patience and self-abandonment, which could not fail to bring blessings and rewards in this world or the next.

(d) A shift of stress in the hierarchy of virtues. 'Even if you say nothing', wrote St. Vincent de Paul, 'if you are really concerned with God, you will touch people's hearts by your very presence.' Father Yves Congar replies, 'History shows that it is not sufficient to be a saint when the world is to be changed; and sanctity often flourishes in the midst of a state of affairs which called urgently for reform'. (True and False Reform in the Church, p. 197.)

These two quotations illustrate another aspect of the contrast between the two spiritualities. One stresses exclusively the value of the interior life, and the other stresses the importance of *prophecy*. With regard to clerics who seek their own salvation in a discarnate recollection, remote from their pastoral responsibilities, Father Michonneau wrote, 'How sad to see men watching a great disaster, and imagining that they are sanctifying themselves, while making no move to arrest it'.

Here is another example. In 1940, during the flight from the Germans, a refugee family was making its way laboriously along the road with an old cart, the man walking in front. In the middle of the night, they arrived in a town where everyone was peacefully asleep. Where were they to knock? Perhaps it would be better to bed down in the cart. Suddenly, a bedroom lit up, and a window opened. 'Who's there?'—a worker in a nightshirt appeared and the situation was briefly explained to him. 'Well, you can't stay there all night, that's certain.' He disappeared from the window. Five minutes later, there was a great commotion in his house, and in the house next door. All the women and children went to sleep in one house, and all the men installed themselves in the other, leaving a whole room free for the refugees. 'What else could we do? They are human beings.'

These working-class people reacted spontaneously in terms of solidarity and humanity. In their place, there are a number of Christians and a number of priests who might have reacted rather according to 'prudence'—'Do you know these people? They may be diseased. Are they worthy of assistance?—One never knows. . . .'

'Some people', wrote Father Michonneau, 'may be in danger of being carried away by an excess of zeal; but if an account were taken of all the priestly lives that have been compromised away, all the priestly energies which have been dissipated, you will find that more wings are broken by an excess of prudence, by the mean arguments of elders, by the negligence of those who fail to canalize the energies of the young, than by intemperate or exaggerated apostolic zeal. There is too much talk of the sins of action, too little of the sins of omission. It is not right for a priest to have as his ideal a life without history, without complication, a life in which everything is arranged by prudent diplomacy—even at the cost of souls.' (*Paroisse, Communauté Missionaire.*)

A priest who preaches about vital contemporary issues is not necessarily a demagogue, or a trouble-maker; he is not necessarily serving political ends, nor is he necessarily a crypto-Communist. The martyrs and the apostles were tried and executed for political subversion; so was Christ Himself. We can see clearly today that this was a mistake, and that they had not in fact left the religious sphere—but was this so clear for the princes and archpriests of their time? The Christian who seeks sanctity must remember that the gospel does not call him to exercises of devotion, but to a conversion of life.

(e) Realism and the sense of humanity. The world of today is particularly sensitive to *incarnate* sanctity. 'Anyone who has talked with the worker-priests is struck by the realism of their priesthood. They may not always respect the traditional forms; but many of our frocked priests who do respect these forms, and follow the rules of the clerical life, are quite incapable of carrying out the work of mediation, however earnest they may be, for the whole social structure cuts them off from the people who must be led back to God.' (*Actualité Religieuse*, 1st October 1953.)

The enemies of the Church are not all saints, and they are not all honest. But it is for us to realize that anti-clericalism has been fostered by our errors, by the spiritual climate we sometimes cultivate which makes our 'pious' members less upright, less generous, less courageous and less magnanimous in their daily lives than many of our adversaries. We have many 'good Christians', pillars of piety, who, by their moral insensitivity, do great harm to the cause of Christianity among unbelievers.

Today, the clergy are going through a period of crisis. They are unable to embrace whole-heartedly the spirituality of incarnation, and yet they are profoundly disatisfied with the spirituality of flight. This is first of all a *pastoral crisis*: 'The young priest arrives full of enthusiasm, with a message to preach; and he meets what I have met—a world of poverty, a world in which it is hardly possible to live even as a man, hardly possible therefore to live as a Christian. Everywhere I am up against problems which cannot be resolved in terms of personal morality'. (*Express*, 12th December 1954.) It is also *a crisis of the interior life.* Generally, the priests who have really made contact with the world of suffering, violence, and disbelief, can no longer feel at ease with the spirituality of flight. They long for a more healthy diet, and can no longer stand the ersatz foods they have been brought up on.

A comparison occurs to me which illustrates this sense of revulsion. We used to sleep in a large communal dormitory. It was warm, and the atmosphere was stuffy. When we went outside, the fresh air woke us up; but when we returned into the dormitory, we found the smell and the heat intolerable. We simply could no longer breathe this air, and we wondered how we could have slept in such an unhealthy atmosphere. We would rather stay outside, and shiver in the cold waiting for breakfast, as long as we could breathe fresh air.

This is what many of us feel about the kind of 'interior life' we were brought up on.

The opposition of the spirituality of flight and the spirituality of incarnation has resulted in a hardening of attitudes on both sides in the conflict over the worker-priests.

(4) *Two forms of apostolate: combat, and dialogue*[6]

The new civilization which has emerged from the nineteenth century is characterized by the predominance of science, and the rapid movement of socialization. These two characteristics of our age merge in 'machinism', the cult of the machine.

The two great movements which have changed the face of the world, the rise of modern science and the emancipation of the proletariat, have both taken place in an atmosphere of fever and passion. Science asserts itself with adolescent arrogance, and the humiliated proletariat still

[6] The encyclical *Mater et Magistra,* which takes a generally favourable view of socialization and Pope John's opening discourse to the Second Vatican Council, which takes a firm stand against the tactics of condemnation, seem to provide an authoritative conclusion to this debate.

trembles with anger. Consequently, this new civilization, which is so full of promise, is troubled by surging passions.

Nineteenth-century Christianity was well able to see the passions and the shortcomings of the two great revolutionary movements; but it was slow to understand their promise. The Church was still influenced by the Christianity of Constantine and of the Middle Ages, and was ill at ease with the new world, which disturbed its ancient modes of thought. She felt that her business was first of all with eternal values, and was embarrassed by the terrestrial preoccupations of the new civilization. She saw in the revolutionary movements only something which threatened her venerable traditions, and incidentally endangered the terrestrial advantages which these traditions had won her.

The Christian reaction was first of all, therefore, a freezing of attitudes in the midst of a world in rapid evolution. Her immobility naturally separated her still further from the moving world, and soon her language, her rules, her enterprises, her thought, her clergy, and her works belonged to a totally different universe from that of the new civilization. The separation of the church from the new world was already complete by the middle of the nineteenth century.

For some time, the progress of history, biblical exegesis, and philosophy took place outside the Christian world, or in contradiction to it. There was no meeting-ground between the pretentious arrogance of the new science and the Christian traditionalists who could only respond by anathema to the new challenges. Catholic thought of the nineteenth century, according to Pope Pius IX, 'still used the oratorical methods of romanticism, while serious thinkers were influenced more and more by the results of the positive sciences, and by the rigour of historical criticism'. The foundations of higher education for Catholics were eventually laid in 1875—half a century too late; for the error of modernism was there to perpetuate the error of the ecclesiastics, and to paralyze the dialogue which Leo XIII had started between theology and modern science.

Once the first panic reaction was over, Christians divided into two parties. One party chose to fight; they were determined to preserve the truth unblemished, and to attack by every means the errors of atheism and materialism. The other tried to find a solution in dialogue.

For the first party, dialogue was impossible; the adversary, they considered, was in bad faith, and any 'dialogue' between a Christian and the enemy would be a dialogue between a simpleton and a rogue. They therefore denounced all such efforts with unmitigated zeal, whatever the calibre of the people involved. In spite of this furious opposition from their brothers in the faith, the 'dialoguers' continued their work. They trusted in scriptural promises—'The Holy Spirit will enable you to understand all things'—and they believed that our present search for understanding could rely, as in the past, on the help of God. They obstinately followed the advice of St. Paul—'Examine all things, and hold fast that which is good'. (1 Thess. v. 21.) They realized that behind the conflict of the worker-priests, and beyond the question of who was in error, there lay the deeper opposition between the 'apostolate of the crusade' and the 'apostolate of dialogue'.

For some Christians, 'socialization' means simply the Marxist view of economy, of the state, or religion, and of man. They set out on their gallant crusade against Marxism, and fight a battle on many fronts—ideological, military, political, spiritual.

There is therefore a 'devout' circle which expresses its love for the working-class, its hunger and thirst for justice, by a systematic hostility to Communism and an external and equivocal devotion to Our Lady of Fatima. The worker-

155

priests were frequently criticized for refusing to take part in this anti-Communist crusade.

The whole world, with its rapidly expanding population, is becoming like a huge machine in which every man has his special *rôle*, a machine which must be continuously improved to ensure greater productivity. Crafts are replaced by big industry, small shops by supermarkets, and general culture has to give way before ever-increasing specialization. We are evolving towards a world in which we shall be less and less able to afford the luxury of private initiative and individual liberty, and in which there will be more and more anonymous officials carrying out automatically an impersonal task under the control of an anonymous administrator, himself with limited responsibility.

We can rejoice in this evolution, or we can deplore it; but whichever we do, we cannot alter the course of history. We are on the way to universal socialization.

The worker-priests were attacked because they believed in this evolution, and tried to carry out a ministry which took full account of social reality.